P9-DMM-030

THE GREAT AND ONLY BARNUM

THE TREMENDOUS, STUPENDOUS LIFE OF SHOWMAN P.T. BARNUM

BY CANDACE FLEMING

ILLUSTRATED BY RAY FENWICK

schwartz & wade books · new york

Visit us on the Web! www.randomhouse.com/kids
Educators and librarians, for a variety of teaching tools,
visit us at www.randomhouse.com/teachers

Library of Congress Cataloging-in-Publication Data
Fleming, Candace.
The great and only Barnum : the tremendous, stupendous life of
showman P. T. Barnum / Candace Fleming.
p. cm.
Includes bibliographical references and index.
ISBN 978-0-375-84197-2 (hc)—ISBN 978-0-375-94597-7 (glb)
1. Barnum, P. T. (Phineas Taylor), 1810–1891—Juvenile literature.
2. Circus owners—United States—Biography—Juvenile literature.
I. Title.
GV1811.B3 F55 2009
791.3092—dc22
[B]
2008045847

The text of this book is set in itc usherwood.
The illustrations were rendered in good old black ink,
then cleaned up on the computer.
Book design by Rachael Cole and Helen Capone

Printed in China
1 3 5 7 9 10 8 6 4 2
First Edition

ACKNOWLEDGMENTS

LADIES AND GENTLEMEN, children of all ages, with delightful derring-do and glitzy grammatical garnishing, I proudly present the wondrous people whose elegance, élan, and able assistance made this miraculous manuscript possible:

THAT DYNAMIC DUO from the Bridgeport, Connecticut, Public Library, Mary Witkowski and Bina Williams, who sorted, sifted, and snapped, ensuring that only the most magnificent photographs grace the pages of this book.

THE STUPENDOUSLY GENEROUS Fred D. Pfening III, who allowed the use of rare and exotic photographs from his extraordinary collection of circus memorabilia.

THAT ARCHIVIST EXTRAORDINAIRE, Erin Foley, who with a preponderance of patience and glorious good cheer guided me for weeks on end through the vast collection of the Circus World Museum.

THE FEARLESS Heidi Taylor, who rushed headlong into the darkest archives of the John and Mable Ringling Museum of Art to emerge time and again with fantastical photos and facts.

THE FANTABULOUS Ray Fenwick, master of ink and pen, for his eye-catching, jaw-dropping calligraphic creations.

THUNDEROUS APPLAUSE to that delectably debonair wonder of the computer world, Michael Fleming, and his charmingly brilliant brother, Scott, who wrestle technical problems with bravery and aplomb.

AND IN THE CENTER RING, tremendous, stupendous applause to the glitteringly glamorous Emily Seife; the properly punctuated Barbara Perris; and the marvelous and magical Maren Greif.

AND LET IT BE DECLARED from sea to shining sea that this book could not have been so cerebrally conceived nor wittily written without the electrifying and edifying editorial skill of the astonishing Ann Kelley and the daring yet delectable design talents of the colossally creative Rachael Cole. There is no other team like them in the world!

CONTENTS

He was P. T. Barnum—known far and wide for his bearded ladies and skeleton collections; his midgets and three-ring circuses; his wax museums, jumbo elephants, dancing bears, and mermaids. But by the time the reporter from the *New York Herald* arrived, P. T. Barnum was an old man. When the reporter was led to the showman's bedroom, she was shocked by his frail appearance. Too tired to leave his Bridgeport, Connecticut, mansion, Barnum now found comfort in watching the gulls outside his window and daydreaming about the upcoming circus season.

"I long to ride with [the circus] once more," he told the reporter.

The reporter felt "an instant kinship" with the old man. She, too, loved the circus—especially the Barnum & Bailey circus. "It always . . . took my breath away," she later admitted. She was here to uncover the *real* P. T. Barnum, so she asked her first question. It was, she later confessed, an "impertinent" one. "Do you ever wish you had done something more important with your life? Do you ever wish you had become a doctor . . . or preached from the pulpit and saved men's souls?"

The jobs the reporter mentioned were certainly more respectable. But were they really more important than Barnum's sixty years in show business? He didn't think so. "Amusement may not be the great aim of life," he finally answered, "but it gives zest to our days."

Barnum had dedicated his life to amusing people. His goal, wrote historian Philip B. Kunhardt, was "to awaken a sleeping sense of wonder, to help open the eyes of his fellow citizens to the amazing diversity of the human and natural world." To do this, he had introduced them to the rare, the strange, the beautiful, and the exotic.

Startling inventions!

Little-known tribespeople!

Fossils, mummies, and three-headed snakes!

All this and much, much more had been Barnum's contribution to nineteenth-century America.

Yet some people called him silly and selfish. They made fun of his museums and circuses, and claimed that his only purpose was to make lots of money.

"He represents everything crass and self-serving in the American character," the famous author Mark Twain once wrote.

What did Barnum say to those critics?

"I am a showman," he replied simply, "and all the gilding shall make nothing else of me."

ONE OF THE LAST PHOTOGRAPHS TAKEN OF
P. T. BARNUM, AT THE AGE OF EIGHTY-TWO.

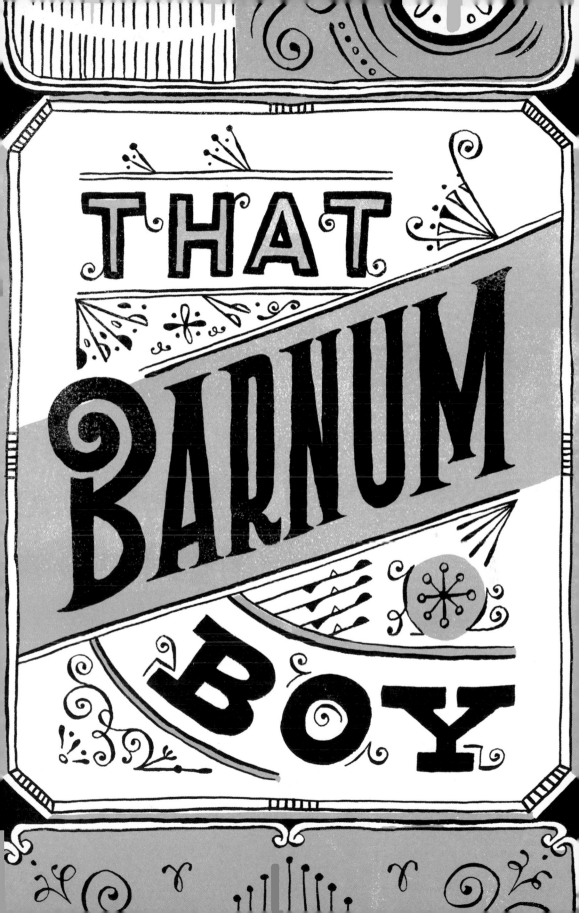

IN 1810, BETHEL, CONNECTICUT, was a tiny village. Pigs ran freely through the dirt streets, and spots in and around town had colorful names like Wildcat Road, Plum Trees, and Toad-Hole. Back then, the village was cut off from the world—newspapers arrived only once a week, and a journey to distant New York was considered a great adventure—so folks had to take care of themselves. Homemade candles lighted houses, and in the summer nearly everyone went to bed as soon as it grew dark, to save wax. They ate what they raised—mostly boiled and baked beans, coarse rye bread, applesauce, and "pot luck," a concoction of corned beef, salt pork, and clams from the nearby coast. Pewter plates were considered "fancy eating" (wooden ones worked just as well), and when one of the richer citizens covered the bare floor in his bedroom with a small piece of carpet, the town buzzed that he was showing off his wealth.

Everyone worked hard. "I can see it as if but yesterday," recalled one villager, "our hard-working mothers . . . spinning, reeling . . . knitting, darning, mending, washing, ironing, cooking, soap and candle making, pluck[ing] the geese,

TALE'S HOMETOWN

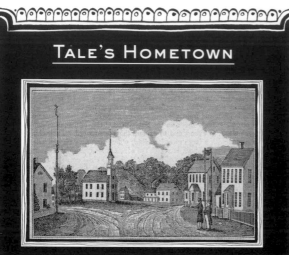

AN ENGRAVING OF BETHEL, CONNECTICUT.

In the center of Bethel stood the most popular place in town, the Congregational church. Sunday after Sunday, villagers shivered in the cold, hard pews, listening to sermons about fire and brimstone. The church was unheated even in the winter, because religious passion was considered warmth enough. The second most popular place in town was the building on the far right. This was the Barnum family's store and tavern, where liquor flowed freely. Drinking was as much a part of Bethel life as sermons. Remembered one old-timer, "Every sort of excuse was made for taking a drink. . . . Even at funerals the clergy, mourners, and friends drank liquor."

milk[ing] the cow, mak[ing] butter and cheese. . . ." The men worked too, plowing, planting, harvesting.

Many of Bethel's farmers had owned their land for generations. There were the Hoyts, the Beebes, the Barnums, and . . . the Taylors. Everyone knew the Taylors, especially Phineas Taylor—Uncle Phin, the townsfolk called him. (It was the custom in those days to call everybody uncle or aunt rather than Mr. or Mrs.) Uncle Phin was the town wag, a cunning, sharp prankster who was always one jump ahead of his friends with puns and practical jokes.

UNCLE PHIN'S MOST FAMOUS PRANK

Once when Uncle Phin was traveling by sailboat with a group of businessmen, the wind died. As the boat sat unmoving for five days, the once clean-shaven men grew scruffy beards. Not one of them had thought of bringing along a razor—except for Phin. When the boat finally began to move again, Phin announced that he had a fair plan to get everyone shaved with just one razor. Each man would shave half his face, then pass the razor on to the next man. When all were half shaved, the rotation would begin again. All went smoothly at first. Phin shaved half his face, then passed the razor on. Eventually, everyone was half shaved and the razor returned to Phin. He finished shaving the second half of his face, then announced that the blade was dull and needed to be sharpened. Since old-fashioned razors were sharpened by striking them against a leather strop, Phin began whipping the blade back and forth. Then—oops!—the razor suddenly flew out of his hand and into the waters of Long Island Sound. Hours later the boat docked in New York, and the sheepish businessmen got off. People on the pier couldn't help gawking at the strange sight. Every man was neatly shaved on one side, whiskered on the other—every man, that is, except for the wildly laughing Phin.

A SKETCH OF
UNCLE PHIN.

A Bit About Tale's Father

"My father, Philo Barnum," wrote Tale, "was a man with a large frame, erect and up-headed. He had bright blue eyes that were well open and intent upon the circumstances surrounding him." Descended from the town's founders, Philo's grandfather had served as a captain during the American Revolution and afterward made a fortune in politics and hotel keeping. By the time Philo was born, the family money was gone and Tale's father could barely make ends meet. During his lifetime he moved through a series of jobs—tailor, tavern keeper, owner of a livery stable, store clerk, and farmer. Not one of these occupations left him financially secure. He had other problems, too. His first wife, Polly Fairchild, died in 1808, leaving him alone with five small children. In good New England fashion, Philo quickly remarried: Six months later, he wed Irena Taylor.

Despite these struggles, Philo seemed to be a hands-on father who insisted Tale could "hoe and plough and dig in the garden as well as anybody else." When he realized his son did not like manual labor, he put the boy to work as a store clerk. And as soon as little Tale began earning some money, his father insisted he begin paying for his own clothing. "I was but seven years old at the time, yet my father did not miss an opportunity for a financial lesson . . . 'Bills must be paid,' he told me then. It is still a painful, but truthful life lesson."

A Bit About Tale's Mother

Little is known about Irena Barnum, but by all accounts she was a quiet, kindly, and self-reliant mother. She was not an openly affectionate woman. "Kisses and hugs were not in her character," Tale once said. Still, she was a good mother who instilled in her son the values of hard work and frugality. "As a small boy my mother taught me that I should save all my pennies, and so I did," Tale said. A devout Christian who attended services in Bethel's meetinghouse twice a week (on Wednesdays and Sundays), Irena had no desire for riches. Later in life, when her son became rich and famous, he repeatedly offered to build her a mansion. But Irena refused. Instead, she quietly lived on in the plain house where she had borne her children. "She loved her little town and her gaggle of relatives," wrote Barnum.

THIS PHOTOGRAPH OF TALE'S MOTHER, IRENA, WAS TAKEN YEARS AFTER HER SON HAD MOVED AWAY FROM BETHEL. NO IMAGE OF TALE'S FATHER EXISTS.

He would, remembered one villager, "go farther, wait longer, work harder and contrive deeper to carry out a [prank] than for anything else under heaven."

In 1810, a baby boy was born into Uncle Phin's joke-loving family. Just the day before, Bethel had celebrated the country's thirty-fourth birthday with parades, picnics, and fireworks. But on the fifth of July, Irena Taylor Barnum (Phin's daughter) gave birth to her first son. Her husband, Philo Barnum, named the boy after his prank-playing grandpa, Phineas Taylor. While the child would eventually grow up to be known the world over as P. T. Barnum, when he was a baby his family simply called him Tale.

Tale never regretted not being a firecracker baby. "I'd have enjoyed being born on the Fourth of July," he later wrote, "but maybe my tardiness was for the best. Competition between Barnum and Independence Day would have been too much. As it was, I made my appearance after peace and quiet had been restored and the audience had [returned to] its seat."

THE BARNUM BUNCH

The Barnum house was bursting with children. There were:
* Rana, born in 1800 (to Philo's first wife, Polly)
* Almon, born in 1801 (to Polly)
* Minera, born in 1803 (to Polly)
* Philo Fairchild, born in 1806 (to Polly)
* Mary H., born and died in 1808 (to Polly)
* Phineas Taylor, "Tale," born in 1810 (to Philo's second wife, Irena)
* Eder, born in 1813 (to Irena)
* Mary, born in 1815 (to Irena)
* Cordelia, born in 1820 (to Irena)
* Almira, born in 1823 (to Irena)

Yet later in life, when Tale wrote his autobiography, *The Life of P. T. Barnum, Written by Himself,* he barely included his siblings in his childhood memories. He didn't describe them, and in many ways he wrote as if he had been an only child. Out of four hundred pages of memoir, Tale told only one story about a sibling. He wrote:

"I usually slept with my younger brother, Eder. Frequently I would join some of our village boys in a party at the house of their parents . . . and at eleven o'clock at night (which was later than my parents permitted) I would slyly creep up the stairs, and crawl into bed with the greatest caution lest I wake my brother, who would be sure to report my late hours to my

. . . CONTINUED ON PAGE 10

As for Uncle Phin (who was now Grandfather Phin), his namesake delighted him. "I was his pet," Tale later remembered, "and during the first six years of my life spent most of my waking hours in his arms. My mother estimates that the amount of lump sugar which I swallowed from his hands during that period could not have been less than two barrels."

But Grandfather Phin gave his namesake something more than sugar. When Tale was two, he deeded the boy a piece of land called Ivy Island. Tale grew up hearing about this property. "My grandfather always spoke of me (in my presence) to the neighbors and to strangers as the richest child in town since I owned the whole of Ivy Island," he later recalled. "My father and mother frequently reminded me of my wealth and hoped I would do something for the family when [I grew up]."

For years little Tale dreamed of his property. He imagined it as a lush green island set in the middle of a sparkling blue lake and covered with gold and diamond mines. Over and over he promised his playmates that when he grew up, they would all live—happily and richly—on Ivy Island.

THE BARNUM BUNCH

. . . CONTINUED FROM PAGE 9

parents. My brother contrived all sorts of plans to catch me on my late return. Sometimes he would pile trunks and chairs against the door, so I would . . . upset the barricade and awaken [my parents] by the noise. I managed, however, to open the door by degrees and get to bed without awakening the slumberers. One night I found the door nailed [shut].

"I descended the stairs, found a short ladder outdoors and entered through our bedroom window without being discovered. Another night, Eder sat up in the middle of the bed and bolstered himself with pillows, determined to keep awake until I returned. But sleep overcame him, and when I arrived I snugged myself cozily into bed and went to sleep. In the morning, he found himself sitting bolt upright in bed, just as he went to sleep the night before. Giving me a kick, he woke me up and exclaimed: 'You worked it pretty well last night, but I'll catch you yet.' 'You are welcome to do it if you can,' I replied, 'but you will have to get up early in the morning to catch a weasel asleep.' For months, Eder kept at it, but he never caught [me]."

MISADVENTURES ON IVY ISLAND

When Tale was twelve, he finally got to see his island. His father walked him out to a nearby meadow called East Swamp and pointed. "There," he said, "where you see those beautiful trees rising in the distance."

Leaving his father behind, Tale headed in that direction. Soon the ground became boggy and wet, and

THIS ENGRAVING DEPICTS TALE ESCAPING FROM IVY ISLAND—INTO THE WAITING ARMS OF HIS FATHER.

the boy found himself struggling through waist-deep water. A cloud of mosquitoes buzzed around his head. Hornets stung him. Still, he pressed on . . . and on . . . and finally he dragged himself up onto a tiny spit of land to discover—a worthless, snake-infested thicket! There were no diamond mines, just a few stunted ivies and some straggling trees. "The truth flashed upon me," said Tale. It had all been a huge practical joke, and "I had been the laughingstock of the family and neighborhood for years."

This cruel joke had been meant to strip Tale of his boyhood dreams and turn him into a hardworking Yankee. Instead, it turned Tale into a prankster and a practical joker. "I became," the boy confessed, a "chip off my grandfather's block."

THE YOUNG BUSINESSMAN

Tale began saving his pennies when he was five years old. When he turned six, Grandfather Phin took him to the village tavern and exchanged "all my little pieces of coin for one dollar." Tale was stunned. "Never had I felt so rich, so absolutely independent of the world, as I did when I looked at that monstrous big silver dollar, and felt that it was all my own."

From that moment on, the boy loved money. And he promised himself that he would make lots of it. At first, Grandfather Phin paid the boy a few cents each day to help with small chores on the farm. But this didn't make Tale's pile of money grow fast enough. So when he was just eight years old, he came up with a surefire way of making money. "I became a peddler," he said. Every third Saturday of the month, volunteer soldiers came to Bethel to train on the village green. Tale began making molasses candy and selling it to the soldiers, who were hungry after all their marching. "I usually found myself a whole dollar richer at the end of training," the boy remarked. Soon he expanded his business. Besides candy, "I began selling ginger bread, cookies, sugar candies and cherry rum. . . . I made a small fortune."

Seeing his son's growing wealth, his father "considerately allowed me to start [paying for] my own clothing," said Tale. "This arrangement kept my pile reduced to a moderate size."

HEAD-WORK

Tale could have added to his fortune by working for his neighbors. Folks were always offering to pay him for cutting hay or mucking out cow stalls. Problem was, Tale hated farmwork. He spent more time finding ways to get out of doing his own chores than simply doing them. "I always disliked work," admitted Tale. "Head-work I was excessively fond of. I was always ready to concoct fun, or lay plans for money-making, but hand-work was decidedly not in my line."

Because he was so good at "head-work," he excelled in school. "I was considered a pretty apt scholar," he bragged. "There [were only] two or three [students] considered my superior."

Tale began attending school at the age of six, and he might have been at the head of his class if he had gone every day. But Tale's father often needed him to help on the farm, so he was kept out of school. Still, by the standards of the day, he was well educated. Not only did he attend the local school, but also, during one summer, his parents sent him to a private academy in nearby Danbury. There he received a good grounding in grammar and handwriting, reading the classics and learning to write essays and poetry.

But Tale's best subject was math. He repeatedly astonished his Bethel teacher by adding up long columns of numbers in his head. Once, Tale was awakened in the middle of the night by his teacher, Zerah Hudson, who had bet a neighbor that the boy could calculate the number of feet in a load of wood in five minutes. While a sleepy Tale stood in the Barnum kitchen wearing nothing but his nightshirt, schoolmaster Hudson called out the problem.

"To the great delight of my teacher, my mother and myself, I gave the result in less than two minutes," boasted Tale.

TALE TALKS ABOUT SCHOOL

While Tale seemed to enjoy learning, he didn't like attending school. Here's all he ever wrote on the subject:

"A schoolhouse in those days was a thing to be dreaded—a schoolmaster, a kind of being to make the children tremble. . . . [My] teachers used the ruler prodigiously (to smack the knuckles of unruly students), and a dark dungeon which was built in the house was occupied nearly all the time during school hours by some unlucky child who had incurred the displeasure of the one-man power."

FRIENDS

"I had plenty of playmates," Tale once wrote. "I never lacked for chums to go swimming or fishing with."

One of these playmates was John Haight, a boy who was always at the center of trouble. John cussed. He stole. He jumped naked off a bridge in front of Sunday's churchgoers.

"Don't you dare play with that John Haight," Tale's mother would warn her son over and over again.

But did Tale obey his mother?

"Absolutely not," he declared. "While I did not dare break any rules myself I loved being a party to the fun and excitement." And hanging around John was always fun and exciting. "I both liked and feared [him]. I liked him for his daredevil sort of character, and feared him because he was a terrible [bully]."

One winter's afternoon, a dozen schoolboys—John and Tale included—went ice-skating on a nearby pond. Reckless as usual, John dashed across the thin ice. The ice cracked, and John fell through.

"Help!" he hollered, clinging to the ice. "Help, or else I'm going to give every one of you a thundering licking when I get out!"

His threat scared the others. Each and every one of them had been "licked" by John before. Fearing he would beat them up as soon as they pulled him out, they quickly skated away, leaving John to fend for himself.

The next morning, Tale was headed to school when John leaped out in front of him. "I could feel his breath upon my face," said Tale, "and looking me square in the eye, he exclaimed, 'Mr. Taylor Barnum, it seems I owe you a licking.'" Then John took off his coat, and "in less than two minutes I was pretty well pummeled."

Tale stumbled home, "drowned in tears."

When he arrived, his mother asked what had happened. Tale told her.

His mother shrugged. "Serves you right for keeping such company," she scolded.

But Tale continued to keep John's company. "He taught me early on that there are consequences when one engages in risky ventures . . . and engaging with John was always risky."

GOING TO CHURCH

Twice a week, Tale attended services at the Congregational church. Members of the Congregational church were Calvinists. They believed that man by nature was sinful; that God had already decided at the beginning of time who would and would not go to Heaven; that good works had no effect on

Every autumn, an unusual couple lumbered into Bethel. It was Hack Bailey and his elephant, Old Bet.

Old Bet was one of the first elephants ever seen in the United States. Hack had bought her from a sea captain in 1815 for $1,000. That was a lot of money. But Old Bet quickly earned it back. Traveling through New England at night so the public wouldn't get a glimpse of the elephant for free, Hack turned up in tiny villages all across Connecticut. He exhibited his pachyderm in barns and on town greens. By charging a small fee to see her up close, he eventually made a huge fortune.

And he left a lasting impression on Tale Barnum. Wide-eyed, the boy listened to Hack's stories of traveling the country, making money with exhibits, and being in the elephant business. The story Tale remembered most vividly, however, had to do with Hack's partner—a man who refused to share Old Bet's profits. Hack's solution was to point an unloaded rifle (he was bluffing, after all) at the elephant and declare, "You may do what you please with your half of the elephant, but I am fully determined to shoot my half." The partner quickly split the profits.

From this story, Tale learned two lessons that he remembered all his life. The first was "learning how to call an adversary's bluff with a threat that cannot be ignored." The second was "When entertaining the public, it is best to have an elephant."

AN ENGRAVING OF HACK BAILEY
AND HIS PARTNER ARGUING OVER
THE FATE OF OLD BET.

those who had already been chosen to burn in Hell. "Many and many a time, I returned home from an evening prayer meeting frightened, and almost smelling, feeling and tasting those everlasting burning waves," recalled Tale. "I could hear the shrieks and groans of children and parents and even aged grandparents. They had lived lives of goodness, yet a wrathful God had committed them to burn. . . . Certainly I could not love such a God."

Around the age of thirteen, Tale turned his back on the stern teachings of his parents and became a Universalist. Unlike the Calvinists, Universalists believed that God's nature was love, and that *all* men and women were destined for Heaven.

Grandfather Phin, who already attended the Universalist meetings in nearby Newtown, helped Tale in his conversion. How Tale's parents felt about their son's religious change has been lost to history. But when one of the Calvinist preachers complained about it, Grandfather Phin angrily declared that their church "might go to the devil."

Tale called his new religion a "cheerful Christianity" and wrote a Sunday-school paper that contained the first seeds of the count-your-blessings, all-things-are-possible, never-look-back philosophy he would come to live by. "The one thing needful," wrote the thirteen-year-old, "is to believe on the Lord Jesus Christ, follow in his footsteps, love God and obey his commandments, love our fellow-man, and embrace every opportunity of administering to his necessities. . . . In short, the one thing needful is to live a life we can always look back upon with satisfaction."

CHANGES

In 1825, when Tale was fifteen years old, his father fell ill with a fever and died. All of a sudden, Tale's childhood was over, and "the world looked dark indeed." After the burial, his family "returned to our desolate home, feeling that we were forsaken by the world, and little hope existed for us this side of the grave."

Things looked even darker when the family learned that Philo Barnum had owed lots of money. Everything the family owned was sold to pay those debts, even the shoes Tale had worn to the funeral. "I was beginning in the world," he said, "and I was barefooted at that."

It was up to Tale—who now liked to be called Taylor—to keep his mother and four younger siblings from starving. So he took a job as a clerk in his uncle's store and moved to Grassy Plain, a mile from Bethel. Taylor wasn't the hardest worker. Instead, he spent lots of time thinking up ways to make money while avoiding work.

One time, Taylor learned of some customers who liked to do their shopping before the sun came up. Since he preferred sleeping in to standing behind the store's counter, he came up with a creative idea. Every night he tied a string around his big toe, hung the other end out his bedroom window, which was above the store, and left a sign telling customers to pull the string for service. When they did, he would leap out of bed, wait on the customers, and then hop back under the covers until the next customer tugged.

Taylor had other clever business ideas, too. One day a traveling salesman arrived at the store and sold Taylor a useless load of small green bottles. Even though they'd been incredibly cheap, his uncle was angry. Who, he demanded, would buy an empty bottle?

But Taylor had a plan. Days later, customers at the store were greeted by a big sign that read:

MAGNIFICENT LOTTERY!
OVER 550 PRIZES!!
ONLY 1000 TICKETS!!!

Customers were thrilled. More than five hundred winners for one thousand tickets? At that rate, every other ticket would be a winner! Recalled Taylor, "Those lottery tickets went like wildfire." At fifty cents apiece, customers sometimes bought a dozen or more tickets at a time, and the young man raked in the money. Finally, the big day arrived. The lucky tickets were drawn, and customers came to claim their prizes. What did they win? The green glass bottles, of course! When the raffle ended, not only were Taylor's bottles gone, but the store was hundreds of dollars richer. As for the customers, they happily carried their prizes home. "People," Taylor learned that day, "like to win, no matter how small the prize."

In 1826, when Taylor was sixteen, he decided Connecticut was too small for his schemes and dreams. So he moved to Brooklyn, New York, to clerk in a grocery store owned by a former neighbor from Bethel. There Taylor learned about business on a larger scale. He attended auctions, discovered how to buy inventory at cheap prices, and learned how to estimate profits.

More importantly, he learned something about himself. He discovered he didn't want to work for someone else and simply be paid a salary. He wanted his own business. What kind? Taylor wasn't sure. But three years later, when Grandfather Phin offered to help him start a business back in Bethel, Taylor jumped at the chance. He quickly packed his bags and went home.

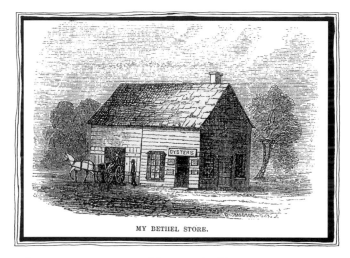

MY BETHEL STORE.

AN ENGRAVING OF TAYLOR'S BETHEL STORE. HIS SPECIALTY WAS OYSTERS, WHICH HE ADVERTISED AS BEING "FRESH THREE TIMES A WEEK."

There was another reason Taylor was eager to return home. Before he had moved to Brooklyn, a girl named Charity Hallett had come into his store shopping for a bonnet. "The view I had of this girl sent all sorts of agreeable sensations through [me]," Taylor later recalled. As she tried on hats, a summer storm blew up. Too scared to ride home by herself, Charity begged the store clerk to escort her. He happily agreed. As they rode side by side on horseback, they talked. "She was friendly," said Taylor, "and not the least bit 'stuck up.'"

Once he was back in Bethel, nineteen-year-old Taylor quickly became reacquainted with Charity, who was now working as a seamstress in town. Soon he considered the girl his "sweetheart" and proclaimed her "one of the best women ever created." The young couple were married on November 8, 1829.

TAYLOR'S WIFE

This portrait of Charity Barnum, made eighteen years after her wedding, is the earliest known picture of her. While it makes her look dour and colorless, the young Charity was full of fun. "She heartily enjoyed [Taylor]," recalled one family friend, "and could not keep her laughter down." She also liked to tease her young husband, much to his delight. "Charity really gave me a stinger that time, didn't she?" he would proudly declare. And Charity would blush, because she loved getting "one up" on the witty Taylor.

Not only did Taylor have a wife to support, but he soon had a child as well. On May 27, 1833, Charity gave birth to their first daughter, Caroline Cordelia. Taylor tried to settle down. In his Bethel store, he sold "all kinds of dry goods, groceries, crockery, etc. 25 per cent cheaper than any of his neighbors." But grocery stores bored him. His restless imagination and boundless energy needed someplace big and bustling; someplace where he could find a challenge and make a fortune; someplace like . . .

New York City!

In the winter of 1834, he packed up his wife and child and headed into his future.

THE BARNUMS ARRIVED IN NEW YORK in the winter of 1834. After renting a small house on Hudson Street, Taylor—who now used his initials, P.T., in his business dealings but preferred to be called Barnum—went about seeking his fortune. Every morning he read the want ads in the *New York Sun,* searching for an interesting job. He wanted one where he could use his imagination and energy. He wanted to be his own boss. And he wanted to make lots of money. But all he found were advertisements for mouse-trap salesmen and store clerks. Once again, Barnum settled for a job in a grocery store.

But he was watching. And listening. And learning. He got one of his most important lessons the same year he moved to the city. That was when the *New York Sun* announced that Sir John Herschel, the world's most famous astronomer, had invented a telescope so powerful, it could actually see life on the moon. Every day for an entire week, the *Sun* reported the incredible details of Herschel's discoveries. Through his telescope, reporters wrote, the scientist had spied unicorns, lunar bison, even a tribe of beavers that lived in huts. The high point of the *Sun*'s coverage came when it revealed that Her-

shel had discovered a race of winged humans called man-bats who lived in a mysterious golden-roofed temple.

Like other New Yorkers, Barnum was fascinated by these discoveries. He pored over the articles, as well as pictures published in the *Sun*.

THIS PICTURE, PRINTED IN THE *NEW YORK SUN*, SHOWED READERS LIFE ON THE MOON.

Nowadays, readers would have recognized the stories as nothing more than tall tales. But because the articles were filled with scientific-sounding evidence, elaborate details, and eyewitness accounts, they sounded like the truth. "It was a simple and very clever way to get people to believe," Barnum noted.

He noticed something else, too. When the truth came out, readers were not angry at the newspaper. Instead, they laughed as if they liked having had the wool pulled over their eyes. "Most people enjoy a harmless hoax," decided Barnum.

But most importantly, he noticed that the moon stories had made the *Sun*—at least for a while—the bestselling newspaper in the country. "A fortune was made with a bit of good-natured deception," said Barnum.

THE WORLD'S OLDEST LIVING WOMAN

All these lessons from the "Moon Hoax" were still fresh in Barnum's mind when the showman Coley Bartram told him about a bizarre exhibit for sale in Philadelphia.

The exhibit was Joice Heth, a slave who looked not just old, but positively ancient. Weighing only forty-six pounds, she was toothless, blind, and almost completely paralyzed. The only parts of her body she could move were one hand, with its four-inch gnarled nails, and her mouth.

Incredibly, Coley claimed, Joice was 161 years old. Torn from her homeland in Africa and sold into slavery, she had eventually become the property of Augustine Washington, the father of George Washington. "I was the first person to put clothes on the infant who was destined in after days to lead our heroic fathers on to glory, to victory, and to freedom," Joice would later tell audiences. "I even nursed him when his mother could not."

It was an astounding story. Barnum, still languishing behind the grocery store counter, was so excited by it, he caught the next stagecoach to Philadelphia. The minute he saw the old woman, he knew he had found a gold mine. But before investing in the exhibit, he demanded proof of Joice's extraordinary age. Immediately, the owners of the exhibition pulled out a crumbling bill of sale signed by Augustine Washington and dated February 5, 1727. It clinched the deal. Barnum bought the rights to the exhibit in August 1835 for $1,000, money he borrowed from friends. Then, bill of sale in hand, he took Joice to New York City.

Did this make Barnum a slave owner? He claimed he had merely "rented" Joice from her real master, who lived in Kentucky. The only thing he owned, he insisted, was the exhibition. But even if he didn't technically own Joice, he still acted like her master. He displayed the tired old woman before the public. And she had no choice but to submit.

In Barnum's day, showmen commonly exhibited unusual people like Joice for money. Some of these exhibits were dehumanizing events where audiences stared and jeered. But others were in a different class. The audience would meet the unusual person in a respectable, respectful setting. The visitors would be given a chance to talk with the person, ask questions, or sing along with hymns. It was this type of exhibit Barnum wanted for the old woman.

Plunging into show business, he plastered New York City with handbills and posters.

He persuaded newspapers to discuss the exhibit in their stories and editorials.

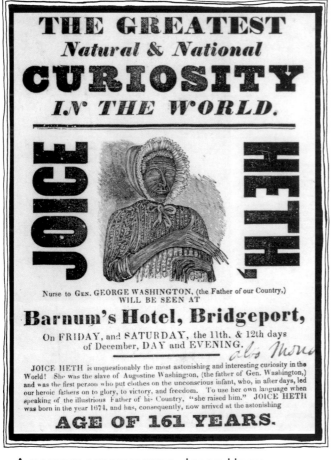

A POSTER ADVERTISING JOICE HETH.

And he hired an amiable and fast-talking friend named Levi Lyman to introduce Joice to the audience and help her answer their questions.

Then he rented an exhibit hall, placed Joice on an elevated cot in the middle, and began selling tickets.

She was an instant hit! The *New York Sun* declared Joice "a renowned relic," while the rival *Star* claimed she looked like "an Egyptian mummy just escaped from the sarcophagus." For eight hours a day, six days a week, visitors came to shake her hand or take her pulse. Some talked with her about her memories of George Washington; some examined the documents that proved her age. Others sang or prayed with her.

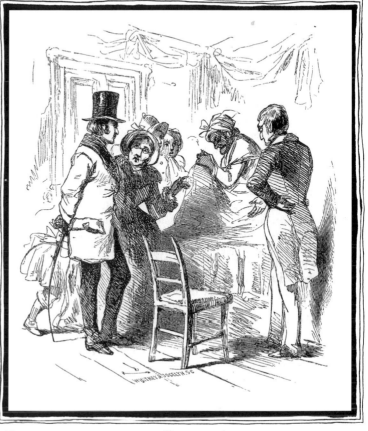

THIS ENGRAVING FROM BARNUM'S AUTOBIOGRAPHY SHOWS JOICE HETH ON DISPLAY.

But all stared as she ate, smoked a pipe, or simply lay on her cot.

Barnum, who was raking in money, was overjoyed with his first success in show business. He claimed to be making $1,500 a week (about $35,000 in today's money). But how did Joice feel? Because she was a slave, no one bothered to record her feelings. Still, one journalist reportedly overheard her begging Barnum to let her go so she could "die and go to glory as a free woman." Her pleas obviously fell on deaf ears. Barnum continued to exhibit her.

Eventually, Joice's novelty wore off and ticket sales dropped. But Barnum had a few tricks up his sleeve. At that time, some shows were exhibiting mechanical mannequins made of rubber and springs. These robotlike machines could be made to move like human beings. So Barnum wrote an anonymous letter to a local newspaper. Wanting to stir up a little controversy, he falsely claimed that Joice was really just a robot and that Barnum was nothing more than a ventriloquist. Crowds who had already paid to view Joice once paid again. They wanted to take another look at the old woman and decide for themselves if she was really a machine. Once again, ticket sales soared. And Barnum learned yet another lesson: "Controversy is good for business."

This success was short-lived. In the late fall, Joice became seriously ill. Barnum sent the old woman to his mother's home in Bethel. There, cared for by a nurse, Joice died on February 19, 1836.

But rumors about Joice kept swirling. Earlier, Barnum had promised to allow a doctor to perform an autopsy on the old woman's body once she died. After all, he figured, someone who could live so long would surely be of interest to science!

He also figured he could make a little more money. After shipping Joice's body back to New York City, he began charging the public a whopping fifty cents (the same price as a good seat at the opera) for one last chance to see the old woman. Incredibly, fifteen hundred people turned out for her dissection.

The autopsy was performed in an amphitheater on Broadway before a vast audience that included doctors, medical students, newspaper reporters, members of the clergy, and other curious citizens. When it was finished, the doctor announced that there had been some mistake about Joice. Far from being 161, she was really no older than 80. The public had been fooled!

Barnum protested that he had been fooled, too. He really *had* believed she was George Washington's nurse. Didn't he have that crumbling bill of sale to prove it?

But gossip was spreading. Some people claimed that Barnum had forced the old woman to memorize the Washington stories. Others asserted that he had pulled out all her teeth to make her look even older. Still others suggested that he had created the ancient-looking bill of sale himself by spitting tobacco juice on it. The *New York Herald* called the Joice Heth episode "one of the most heinous hoaxes ever imposed on an incredulous community," and the mayor of New York declared, "We have been duped!" From that time on, Barnum's name would be linked with hoaxes and fakery.

Later in his career, Barnum often exhibited things he knew were fake. But had he really meant to fool the public this time? No one knows for sure. Still, his experience with Joice Heth opened the door to a field he loved: show business. "I could not imagine doing anything else," he said.

THE TRAVELING SHOWMAN

Not long after the Joice Heth episode, Barnum looked to Aaron Turner, a Danbury neighbor who owned a small traveling show called Turner's Old Columbian Circus, for his next moneymaking scheme. After sending Charity and Caroline back to Bethel to live with his mother, Barnum signed up with

HAWKERS AND WALKERS

In the mid-1800s, people with rare talents, unusual performing skills, or unique exhibits crisscrossed the United States. Puppet shows, bearded ladies, animal acts, medicine men, and trapeze artists all performed for audiences in taverns, inns, and barns. Most of these exhibitors traveled alone and took along only what could be easily transported: a puppet stage, a kaleidoscope, a couple of camels, an owl. Among them was Signor Antonio, a juggler whose specialty was spinning plates, and Professor Cosmo, who played a fiddle while his "educated dog" danced on hind legs. These traveling performers were called hawkers and walkers, and they brought both entertainment and culture to towns all across the country.

this circus. For the next six months, he traveled across the country, selling tickets in return for a piece of the show's profits. And even though it was small—just a magician, a horse that did a few tricks, and a juggler—it made money. At the end of his tour, Barnum walked away with enough cash to set up his own traveling show.

Barnum easily hired some talent, and then he hit the road. Although his troupe was nothing more than a ragtag group of musicians, a juggler, and a clown, he loftily called it Barnum's Grand Scientific and Musical Theater. For the next two years, this troupe traveled across Alabama, South Carolina, and Virginia, singing, dancing, and doing magic tricks beneath a small tent. Once, when his singer ran off from the show, Barnum gamely stepped onstage and sang. He was so good, the audience demanded an encore. Another time, Barnum filled in for a magician who had deserted him. All went well until he tried to pull a squirrel out of his hat. The squirrel bit him. "I shrieked with pain," he remembered, "and overthrew the table, smashed every breakable article upon it, and rushed behind the curtain." The audience demanded its money back.

By the spring of 1838, Barnum was tired of the traveling life. He wanted to spend time with his family. (He hadn't seen his wife and child in close to two years.) He also wanted to start a "respectable, permanent business." So he invested his life's savings—$2,500— in Mr. Proler's (no one knows his

MR. PROLER'S SECRET RECIPE FOR BEAR'S GREASE
(MADE WITHOUT THE BEAR!)

Three pounds of hog's lard and one and a half pounds of mutton tallow. Melt them well together. Then mix, in a separate cup, two ounces each of oil of cloves and oil of bergamot, and one ounce each of oil of lavender, thyme and rosemary. Pour them all into the melted grease, and mix and stir them well together.

P.S. This is the real "Genuine Bear's Grease," which will cover a bald head with beautiful, glossy, curly hair—as quickly as any recipe yet discovered.

first name) cologne, bear grease, and paste-making business. Using Proler's secret ingredients and formulas, Barnum made and sold the goods from a newly opened store at 101-1/2 Bowery in New York City. But business wasn't good, and the store's debts grew . . . and grew . . . and grew. That was when Mr. Proler skipped the country, leaving Barnum with thousands of dollars in unpaid bills and some worthless secret formulas.

Broke, Barnum now turned to a variety of jobs, from tending bar to selling Bibles. But they all seemed too tame. At the age of thirty, P. T. Barnum had a gift for entertaining people and an instinct for promotion. A fast talker, full of jokes, he understood people.

He knew what caught their fancy and piqued their curiosity. He knew how to get them to reach into their pockets, smack down money, and buy a ticket. All he needed was a place to use these special talents—a place like . . .

JOHN SCUDDER'S AMERICAN MUSEUM

Scudder's American Museum sat on the corner of Ann Street and Broadway—the busiest, most important street in New York City. Known as the Great Avenue, Broadway was always very crowded with horses, carriages, wagons, and pedestrians. It should have been one of the best spots for a successful business.

But by 1841, Scudder's was floundering. Opened in 1795, the museum had displayed things such as rocks, plants,

ST. PAUL'S CHURCH AND THE BROADWAY STAGES.
Typical of conditions in the 1830's and 1840's.

THE CORNER OF BROADWAY AND ANN, WHERE SCUDDER'S MUSEUM (FAR LEFT) STOOD ACROSS THE STREET FROM ST. PAUL'S CHURCH.

stuffed birds, and animal skeletons, and people had flocked to see its exhibits. But they soon grew bored with the same dull shelves full of seashells and fossils. Over the years, fewer and fewer people had paid the admission price. Now it was unknown and unnoticed. It was also bankrupt. The museum's owners put the place up for sale.

THIS PAINTING, DONE IN THE 1840s, SHOWS A YOUTHFUL, VIGOROUS BARNUM AT THE START OF HIS CAREER.

Barnum had visited Scudder's before and believed that with a bit of imagination and some creative flair, he could turn the dusty museum into one of New York City's greatest wonders. He decided to buy it.

"You?" snorted a friend when he heard Barnum's plan. "What do you intend buying it with?"

"Brass," replied Barnum, "for silver and gold I have none."

And that's exactly what he did. Though he was penniless, he boldly asked the owner, Francis Olmsted, if he could buy the museum on credit. Barnum promised to make monthly payments until he had paid for the entire place. Then the museum would be his.

Mr. Olmsted admired the young man's bold approach, as well as his business sense. Still, there was a problem. Mr. Olmsted couldn't sign over the museum's deed unless Barnum could put up some sort of collateral—that is, Mr. Olmsted needed some property as a guarantee that he would get his money back if things didn't go as Barnum planned.

MUSEUMS NOW AND THEN

Nowadays, most museums are large public institutions created for the purpose of educating people about specific areas of interest such as art, science, and natural history. Experts run these museums. They are well organized. And their information is accurate.

But in Barnum's day there were no large public museums. Instead, museums were owned by individuals who set up their own displays, then charged the public an admission price. The first person in America to do this was Charles Willson Peale, painter, inventor, and nature enthusiast. Peale founded a museum in Philadelphia in 1784 with the purpose of "bringing together objects that might be helpful in advancing knowledge." He tried hard to create scholarly exhibits. Natural history displays such as stuffed birds and reptile skeletons were arranged according to scientific principles, and some specimens were even placed in replicas of their natural habitats. "Can the imagination conceive anything more interesting than such a museum?" Peale asked. Other would-be museum owners soon began imitating Peale. By the beginning of the nineteenth century, almost every major city had such an establishment.

But these museums soon faced stiff competition from other forms of

. . . CONTINUED ON PAGE 32

amusement. Small circuses, touring artists, and theaters began grabbing the public's interest. People stopped coming to the museums, with their quiet, never-changing, educational exhibits. Museums tried to evolve with the times. Even Peale added "curiosities," such as a two-headed calf and a chip from Queen Victoria of England's chair. But it wasn't enough to recapture the public's attention. By 1840, most of the country's museums were going bankrupt.

That's when Barnum stepped in. Fun came first, and the showman looked for displays that appealed to popular tastes, adding them to his collection in a hodgepodge: giant balls of string next to fossils; ancient coins next to a flea circus. Some artifacts were fake, others were labeled incorrectly, and none included any information about their historical or cultural significance. Later, to compete with theaters and traveling artists, he added live performers, a zoo, and even an aquarium. Americans had never seen anything like it. Wrote the historian A. H. Saxon, "Barnum changed the meaning of the word *museum* in the mid-nineteenth century. Now it had become the name for any building that contained a variety of exhibits and entertainments."

"If only you had a piece of real estate," Mr. Olmsted said.

And Barnum thought: Ivy Island.

"I have five acres in Connecticut," he said. He didn't bother to explain that it was five acres of snake-infested swampland.

"Indeed!" exclaimed Mr. Olmsted. "It [must be] valuable."

Barnum said nothing.

And Mr. Olmsted signed over the deed to the museum.

Later, Barnum wrote with an obvious snicker, "Thus the largest part of my fortune was built on the biggest practical joke of my childhood."

Now Barnum's life centered around the museum. He even lived there, moving Charity, Caroline, and his newest daughter, one-year-old Helen Maria, into a dreary ground-floor apartment that had once been a pool hall. "It saved all sorts of money," said Barnum.

He also saved money by scrimping on meals. Not long after selling the museum, Mr. Olmsted called on Barnum. He found the showman in his office, frugally eating a cold beef sandwich. "I have not eaten a warm dinner since I bought [this place]," Barnum proudly told Olmsted, "and I intend never to eat another . . . until I am out of debt."

After renaming the place Barnum's American Museum and borrowing what he called "start up funds" from his friends, he developed a three-part business plan. First, he would renovate, making the museum cheerful and interesting. Second, he would advertise so people would be intrigued enough to visit. And last but not least, he would fill the museum with fascinating, exciting, ever-changing exhibits. "I had no small plans," admitted Barnum, "and I did not intend to do anything in a small way. To make big

FILLING A MUSEUM

When Barnum bought Scudder's Museum, he also bought the contents. But the old and dusty collections of shells and stuffed animals desperately needed some freshness and variety. So Barnum turned to Peale's Museum in New York. Like Scudder's, Peale's Museum had fallen on hard times, and the owners were eager to sell off its collection. In just weeks, Barnum added insect, fossil, and arrowhead collections, animal skeletons, mounted skins, and several paintings of famous Americans. There was also a great ball of hair that had been found in the belly of a sow, a living cow with five legs and two tails, and the preserved arm and hand of the pirate Tom Trouble. Throughout the next decade, Barnum would continue to buy the contents of other museums—the

Baltimore Museum in 1845, New York City's Chinese Museum in 1846, and finally Peale's Philadelphia Museum in 1848, which landed him the country's only mastodon skeleton.

Because Barnum wanted people to visit his museum again and again, he also set out to hire a parade of constantly changing entertainments. He scoured the country, he later said, for "anything and everything that might bring people into the building." Among his attractions were "industrious fleas, automatons, jugglers, ventriloquists, living statuary, gypsies, albinos, fat boys, rope-dancers . . . puppet shows, fancy glass-blowing and knitting machines." Inside his museum, he claimed, lay "the mysterious and wondrous spectacle of the world."

money, one must always think and act in big ways. It was the world's way then, as it is now."

The showman was true to his words. Four weeks later, his museum opened big, and it stayed big. It held the public's interest fifteen hours a day, six days a week, for the next twenty years.

What made Barnum's American Museum such a popular attraction?

Nothing less than his imagination!

VISITORS TO THE CORNER OF BROADWAY and Ann Street were dazzled and delighted. The once-drab outside walls of Scudder's Museum were covered with huge, brightly colored plaques. After weeks of secret preparation, Barnum had ordered workers to hang the plaques in a single night. Now, on January 1, 1842, the museum's opening day, polar bears, elephants, ostriches, and gorillas loomed from their plaques over Broadway. "It is a fairyland!" exclaimed one spectator.

But that wasn't all. From the museum's roof flew colorful flags of countries around the world, whose flapping could be seen a mile away. Even more amazing was an enormous rooftop lamp—the first spotlight in New York City. When it was turned on, a huge beam of light created by a block of burning lime inside its diamond-shaped lens swept up and down, lighting the streets with a glare as "bright as day."

And then there was the second-story wraparound balcony. Here a brass band played . . . *badly.* Barnum had hired the worst musicians on purpose. He wanted their playing to be so awful that people would pay the admission price just to get away from them. When people complained about the "screeching racket," Barnum just shrugged. "What else do you expect for nothing?" he replied.

Barnum had other ways of bringing people into the museum. He held hot-air balloon ascensions during the day and fireworks displays at night. He installed a gigantic fountain that shot water hundreds of feet into the air, and he invented a way of projecting images onto the museum's outer walls that made the place look as if it were boiling and bubbling. "If it is this wondrous on the outside," declared one museumgoer, "imagine what it must look like on the inside."

Eagerly, people paid their twenty-five-cent admission price and stepped through the doors.

TWO VIEWS OF THE AMERICAN MUSEUM: THE FIRST (OPPOSITE) MUCH AS IT LOOKED ON OPENING DAY, COMPLETE WITH ANIMAL PLAQUES AND FLAGS; THE SECOND (ABOVE) SHOWING THE BADLY PLAYING BAND ON THE BALCONY.

MAKING MONEY

Barnum's American Museum was an instant success. Hundreds of people crowded into the place on opening day—and every day afterward. "For the first year of operation I had planned to spend all my profits on advertising and acquiring performers," remembered Barnum. "The money came in so fast, however, that I was hard pressed to find ways to use it all." In its first year alone, the museum made a profit of $28,000 (about $770,000 in today's money). By 1853, annual profits were $136,000 (almost $3.5 million). And by 1864, they were $300,000 a year (a whopping $4.5 million in today's dollars).

One reason the museum was so successful was that it attracted people from all walks of life. Its low admission price of twenty-five cents put it within reach of the poor and working classes, while its educational displays and lectures appealed to the wealthy. Even immigrants who did not know English flocked to the museum. "One need not speak the native tongue of this great country to enjoy my exhibits," Barnum boasted.

THE COVER AND FRONTISPIECE OF THE AMERICAN MUSEUM'S GUIDEBOOK. THE SKETCHES FOUND INSIDE THIS BOOK ARE THE ONLY IMAGES OF THE MUSEUM'S SALOONS. BARNUM SEEMS TO HAVE PURPOSELY KEPT PHOTOGRAPHERS OUT OF THE PLACE. WORD OF MOUTH, AFTER ALL, WAS HIS BEST RECOMMENDATION, ALONG WITH WRITTEN ADS AND ILLUMINATED BANNERS THAT COULD EXAGGERATE THE EXHIBITS FOUND INSIDE.

THE ENTRANCE HALL

In a gaslit, marble-floored hall, vendors stood hawking a special 112-page illustrated guide to the museum for a dime. "Every visitor should own one," asserted Barnum. Otherwise museumgoers might have a hard time finding their way through his "treasure trove of curiosities."

Barnum's museum was arranged by halls, or saloons, as he called them. There were seven saloons in all, mimicking the "Seven Great Wonders of the

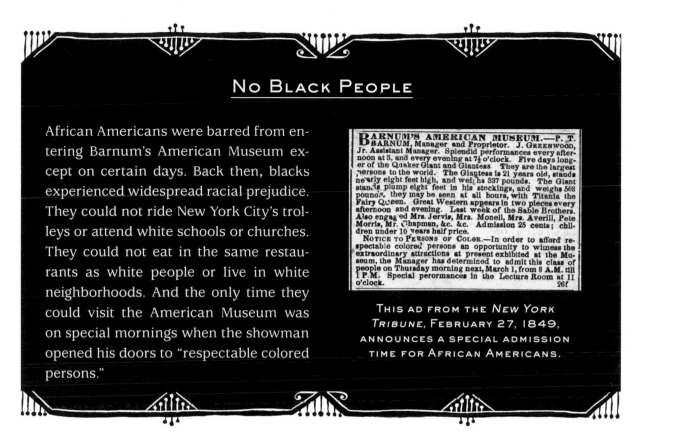

NO BLACK PEOPLE

African Americans were barred from entering Barnum's American Museum except on certain days. Back then, blacks experienced widespread racial prejudice. They could not ride New York City's trolleys or attend white schools or churches. They could not eat in the same restaurants as white people or live in white neighborhoods. And the only time they could visit the American Museum was on special mornings when the showman opened his doors to "respectable colored persons."

BARNUM'S AMERICAN MUSEUM.—P. T. BARNUM, Manager and Proprietor. J. GREENWOOD, Jr. Assistant Manager. Splendid performances every afternoon at 3, and every evening at 7½ o'clock. Five days longer of the Quaker Giant and Giantess. They are the largest persons in the world. The Giantess is 21 years old, stands nearly eight feet high, and weighs 337 pounds. The Giant stands plump eight feet in his stockings, and weighs 508 pounds, they may be seen at all hours, with Titania the Fairy Queen. Great Western appears in two pieces every afternoon and evening. Last week of the Sable Brothers. Also engaged Mrs. Jervis, Mrs. Monell, Mrs. Averill, Pete Morris, Mr. Chapman, &c. &c. Admission 25 cents; children under 10 years half price.
NOTICE TO PERSONS OF COLOR.—In order to afford respectable colored persons an opportunity to witness the extraordinary attractions at present exhibited at the Museum, the Manager has determined to admit this class of people on Thursday morning next, March 1, from 8 A.M. till 1 P.M. Special performances in the Lecture Room at 11 o'clock. 26f

THIS AD FROM THE *NEW YORK TRIBUNE*, FEBRUARY 27, 1849, ANNOUNCES A SPECIAL ADMISSION TIME FOR AFRICAN AMERICANS.

World." While each saloon had a general theme, Barnum often put completely unrelated objects into the exhibits. Beside a display of stuffed birds, for example, a visitor might notice a suit of armor. Next to a glass case of arrowheads, one might find a magnet demonstration. The showman understood that mixing things up made the museum more interesting. It also helped sell the 112-page books.

Guidebooks in hand, visitors now stepped into the first Grand Saloon.

THE FIRST GRAND SALOON

At Barnum's request, carpenters and artists had filled this room (known as the Cosmorama Saloon) with row after row of face-sized windows called cosmoramas—194 in all! Each window opened onto a tiny, lit-up scene of a famous place or historical event. Visitors could peek into the King of France's bedroom, sail down a Venetian canal, or cross the Delaware River with George Washington.

THE FIRST SALOON, OR COSMORAMA.

Afterward, visitors headed to the huge central staircase at the rear of the room. This led to . . .

THE SECOND GRAND SALOON

The second saloon contained an odd assortment of exhibits. Visitors saw not only the Birds of North America collection but also oil paintings of generals, pirates, and other famous people.

In one corner stood a huge stuffed elephant. This was Old Bet, the pachyderm once owned by Barnum's childhood friend Hack Bailey.

Also tucked away in the room's dark corners, for surprise effect, were Barnum's Human Curiosities—people who were, in some way, other than normal. They were, he once said, "representatives of the wonderful," and over the years he employed hundreds of them. Unlike Joice Heth, these performers came to Barnum's museum of their own free will. Some appeared at the museum for only a few weeks, while others stayed for years. In those days, not many people were willing to hire a person with such unique characteristics. Displaying themselves in shows and museums was one of the few ways they could earn a living. And at Barnum's museum the Human Curiosities earned a good one. Not only were they paid generous salaries for the era (anywhere from twenty-five to sixty dollars a week, depending on their popularity with the public), but in many cases they also received a percentage of the museum's ticket sales. Additionally, Barnum provided food and housing for his performers. At any time, giants, bearded ladies, and fat men could be found living in upstairs apartments at the museum. After 1860, most of these Human Curiosities also added to their income by selling souvenir photographs of themselves for fifteen cents apiece. These photographs, called cartes de visite, were popular with museumgoers. Here are some of the Human Curiosities visitors might have seen during the years the museum was open:

The Highland Mammoth Boys. The Highland Mammoth Boys, as they called themselves, were three brothers from Scotland. Together they weighed over 750 pounds. Arriving at Barnum's museum in 1842, they played the bagpipes, wore kilts, danced, and told stories from the "old country." In later years, Barnum's Human Curiosities exhibit was never without a "fat boy."

THE HIGHLAND MAMMOTH BOYS.

Madame Josephine Clofulia. In March 1853, Madame Josephine Clofulia, the celebrated "Swiss Bearded Lady," came to work at the museum. Madame Clofulia had been born with a medical condition that caused excessive hair to grow on her face. Her whiskers first appeared when she was a baby, and they had been left uncut since. By the time the twenty-two-year-old woman arrived at the museum, she had a thick, dark five-inch beard. Visitors often wanted to tug it to see if it was real. Madame Clofulia always refused. "I am a lady," she huffed. "I beg you not to forget that." In case they did, she kept a brooch that showed a portrait of her heavily bearded husband, Monsieur Fortune Clofulia, pinned to her dress.

Chang and Eng. The Siamese twins Chang and Eng were born bound together stomach to stomach. Instead of seeing this as a disability, however, the twins viewed it as extraordinary. In 1829, at the age of eighteen, they left their native Siam (today called Thailand) with hopes of becoming rich and famous in America. Their dreams came true. Traveling from exhibition to exhibition, the twins

MADAME CLOFULIA.

CHANG AND ENG.

generated excitement wherever they went. And for six weeks in 1860, they appeared at the American Museum. Crowds flocked to meet them. "The lines have never been longer," crowed Barnum.

Anna Swan. When Anna was born, she weighed an incredible eighteen pounds. By the time she was three, she already stood four feet, six inches tall. At the age of eight, Anna was her mother's size (five feet, four inches). And by her seventeenth birthday in August 1862, she was nearly full grown at seven feet, eleven inches. That year she went to work for Barnum. The showman gave her an apartment upstairs from the museum, arranged for a private tutor, and had beautiful clothes made especially for her. The softspoken

ANNA SWAN HOLDING AN UNIDENTIFIED CHILD IN THE PALM OF HER HAND.

CAUGHT LOOKING

While the idea of gawking at people with disabilities is repugnant nowadays, in Barnum's day it was a respectable form of entertainment for everyone, including women and children. Barnum took this long-standing tradition of exhibiting Human Curiosities one step further. He wanted the viewers and performers to talk with one another. In his museum, Human Curiosities walked freely about the exhibits, shaking hands with visitors and answering their questions. Sometimes they lectured the audience about their unusual bodies or demonstrated their ability to perform everyday activities. "I want folks to say 'what an amazing person,'" Barnum once declared, "not 'there but for the grace of God go I.'"

giantess was a favorite with the public. And her knowledge of giants (she talked about giants through history, and gave a scientific explanation for her own excessive growth) made her a valued speaker in the museum's lecture hall. Said Barnum, "She is an extraordinary specimen of magnified humanity."

ISAAC SPRAGUE.

Isaac Sprague. Isaac Sprague was a normal, active child until the age of twelve, when he began losing weight. His parents took him to doctor after doctor, but no one could figure out why he was withering away. By the time Isaac was twenty-four, he stood five feet, six inches tall but weighed just forty-four pounds. Too weak to hold a regular job, he turned to show business in 1865. Calling himself the Living Skeleton, he became a popular attraction at Barnum's.

Walking through twin archways, visitors left the Human Curiosities behind and entered . . .

THE THIRD GRAND SALOON

Here visitors could view Barnum's display of stuffed fish, his gem collection, his Native American artifacts, an Egyptian mummy, and a full-scale, accurate model of a Russian fort. Here, too, was the showman's wax museum, with its figures of notable people like Napoleon, Queen Victoria, George Washington, and Jesus Christ. Also on exhibit was a working steam engine made entirely of glass so people could see its inner mechanisms, as well as a hall of mirrors. And in a shadowy corner of the room sat

Madame Dubois, the fortune-teller who would predict a person's future for just twenty-five cents.

But the most popular exhibit in the third saloon was P. T. Barnum himself; his office was tucked between the waxworks and the mirrors. He was as much an attraction as Anna Swan or Chang and Eng. Over the years, Barnum's fame had grown along with the museum's, and by 1845 he already enjoyed a unique public reputation. "The name P. T. Barnum is synonymous with the curious, the wondrous, the odd," the *New York Sun* declared that year. "If it is bold, it is Barnum. If it is big, it is Barnum. As a showman, he stands alone." Barnum encouraged this reputation. He knew that the name P. T. Barnum drew crowds, and he made sure to include it in every handbill, every banner, and every newspaper ad.

Some visitors bought a ticket, marched up to Barnum's office, looked in the door, and left satisfied. The Prince of Wales even visited the museum. He was disappointed to learn that the showman was out of town. "We have missed the most extraordinary curiosity in the establishment," the prince complained.

After peeking into the showman's office, visitors headed to the opposite side of the floor and into . . .

THIS ENGRAVING SHOWS BARNUM AT HIS DESK AT THE AMERICAN MUSEUM. HE BECAME ONE OF THE MOST POPULAR ATTRACTIONS IN HIS ESTABLISHMENT.

An advertisement for Old Neptune.

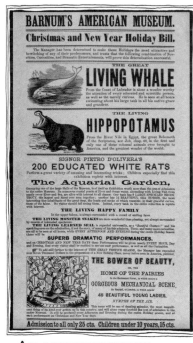

An advertisement for two big exhibits, Barnum's beluga whale and his "behemoth" hippopotamus.

Here visitors found America's first public aquarium, built in 1849. In forty glass and marble cases swam a rainbow of tropical fish. There were sharks and a six-foot electric eel, as well as a live crocodile, dozens of lizards, and "turtles of varying types and sizes." Old Neptune, Barnum's famous Pacific sea lion, lived here, too. Described in the guidebook as "the most Majestic, Terrific, yet docile inhabitant of the Great Deep," Old Neptune could balance a ball on the end of his nose, play a tune on his tin horn, and clap for fish scraps tossed by the audience. When he wasn't performing, he rested in his own private tank.

In the 1860s, Barnum decided to expand his aquarium by adding a hippopotamus. Because hippos need a very large and watery environment, none had ever been seen in America. But Barnum was determined to display one. He built a special habitat based on suggestions from scientists, then had a full-grown hippo shipped from Egypt. Proclaimed Barnum's ads: "This greatest wonder of the animal kingdom should be seen by every man, woman and child!" For months after the hippo's arrival, the museum was crammed with people taking Barnum's advice.

In the middle of the hippo hoopla, the showman learned that Canadian fishermen had caught a beluga whale. No one had seen one in captivity before, so Barnum had it shipped to New York and placed in a brick holding tank in the museum's basement. Thousands came to see the whale, but within days tragedy struck. Because he knew nothing about how belugas lived, Barnum had filled the tanks with fresh water instead of salt water. The animal died. So Barnum built a second tank. Learning from his mistake, he had salt water pumped into it directly from New York harbor. Then he fitted out a sailing expedition to the mouth of the St. Lawrence River, where he personally supervised the capture of a new pair of belugas. These animals adapted successfully to the museum's environment.

From the aquarium, visitors again climbed the grand staircase, this time to the third floor, and stepped inside . . .

THE FIFTH GRAND SALOON

The fifth saloon was filled with stuffed animals: lions, black bears, rhinos, and more. And it was here that the museum offered one of its strangest services. Visitors whose pets had recently died were encouraged to bring the remains of "their dear one" with them to the museum. Once in the fifth saloon, they could leave the animal's body with one of the dozens of taxidermists employed by Barnum. A few hours later, they could return to the saloon to pick up their pet's remains, "freshly mounted and looking as natural as ever."

Here also, in large glass cases arranged along the walls, was an assortment of natural curiosities: butterfly wings, sharks' teeth, animal horns. Nearby was Barnum's

THIS PHOTOGRAPH OF THE MUSEUM'S SURVIVING SPECIMEN CASES—TAKEN WHEN THEY WERE LATER DONATED TO TUFTS UNIVERSITY—PROVIDES A RARE GLIMPSE INTO THE WAYS IN WHICH BARNUM'S COLLECTIONS MIGHT HAVE BEEN DISPLAYED.

Rogues' Gallery, a collection of photographs of some of the world's most notorious criminals.

In the middle of it all stood the museum's refreshment stand. For a nickel, visitors could revive themselves with a glass of lemonade, a bowl of ice cream, or even a plate of steamed oysters. Once refreshed, they moved on to . . .

THE SIXTH GRAND SALOON

The sixth saloon housed a group of unrelated oddities. There were insect collections, ivory carvings, whistles made from pigs' tails, scraps of cloth from Revolutionary War uniforms, minerals, seashells, even a dog working a sewing machine!

After seeing all this, visitors were ready to enter the last saloon. But before doing so, they could take a break from the exhibits by going to a show at . . .

THE MORAL LECTURE HALL

The lecture hall was really a theater, complete with stage, orchestra pit, and seating for three thousand. Barnum, however, refused to call it a theater. In the mid-1800s, respectable people stayed away from theaters because they were filled with hooting, swearing, spitting mobs. "Theaters are places of the devil," warned the famous preacher Henry Ward Beecher. "Avoid them like the plague."

Barnum didn't want people to avoid his theater, so he called it the Moral Lecture Hall. And he made sure that performances on his stage were wholesome, fun, and sometimes even educational. Among the hundreds of performers who appeared on his stage over the years were puppeteers, gymnasts, ballet dancers, and guest lecturers who spoke on such varied subjects as the evils of alcohol, trapping lions in Africa, and creating your own rock garden. There were singers, comedians, jugglers, and Shakespearean actors.

~ INTERIOR VIEW OF THE LECTURE ROOM OF THE AMERICAN MUSEUM, NEW YORK.

THE MORAL LECTURE HALL.

Barnum's lecture hall made the theater something it had never been before: a place for *family* entertainment.

Now visitors climbed the stairway one last time. They headed to the roof, where perhaps the most breathtaking exhibits in the museum awaited.

THE SEVENTH GRAND SALOON

There on the top floor, under open skylights, beside a bubbling fountain, and beneath a canopy of hanging plants and vines, lived Barnum's animals.

Besides the usual lions, tigers, and ostriches, Barnum had a rhinoceros; four giraffes, which he called camelopards; and a pair of prairie dogs. He also owned a gentle orangutan named Fanny. Unlike the other animals, Fanny was not caged and would often leap into visitors' arms and kiss their cheeks.

Here, too, was where the legendary Grizzly Adams and his California Menagerie performed. Adams, a hunter and trapper from the Sierra Nevada, had come to Barnum's museum with several wolves, a half dozen mountain lions, four buffalo, two elk, and twenty immense grizzly bears. The most famous of these bears was Old Sampson, who had been trained to be as gentle as a kitten. While awed audiences looked on, Adams rode Sampson, danced with him, and even stuck his head in Sampson's mouth.

One of the saloon's most intriguing exhibits was the Happy Family. This large collection of natural enemies—cats and rats, owls and mice, eagles and rabbits, with a couple of monkeys and an armadillo thrown in for good measure—had been trained to live together in the same cage. Remarked one museumgoer after peeking into the exhibit, "These animals . . . may have been happy, but they didn't smell nicely."

P. T. BARNUM, ZOOKEEPER

Although Barnum caged all kinds of animals, his menagerie was not well cared for by modern zoo standards. His attitude toward the animals—he simply replaced them when they died—seems cruel nowadays. But in the nineteenth century, little was known about the exotic animals at the museum. No one knew what they ate or how much space they needed. Zoology (the study of animals) was a brand-new science at this time. Scientists were just beginning to understand the animal kingdom. They were still learning about animal habitats and beginning to appreciate the beauty and diversity of the natural world. Barnum helped in this learning process. While he always claimed he didn't know a "clam from a codfish," he eventually earned a reputation among scientists as a great zoologist. Not only did he observe his animals closely, but he also compared their physical characteristics, noted their habits and behaviors, and made educated decisions based on this information. He also wrote to many leading scientists and naturalists. Once in a while he asked them for advice, but more often they turned to Barnum for answers. When the American Museum of Natural History in New York City acquired a baboon, the famous scientist Louis Agassiz asked Barnum how to care for it. "Build the ape a warm cage," replied the showman, because "in my experience apes have a tendency to catch cold." When his animals died, Barnum gave the skeletons and hides to scientific institutions for further study. Even today, his gifts can be seen in the collection of the Smithsonian Institution, as well as at the American Museum of Natural History, the Peabody Museum at Yale University, and Harvard's Museum of Comparative Study.

The seventh saloon's final exhibit was one of Barnum's favorites—his Grand Skeleton Chamber. Here visitors could compare a human skeleton to that of a horse, a hippopotamus, or a mastodon.

After seeing everything, many visitors didn't want to leave. They wanted to stay all day and see it all again. But this caused problems. Not only did the museum get too crowded, but also the line outside grew and grew. It snarled traffic so badly on Broadway that the police repeatedly complained.

That was when Barnum got a brilliant idea. He made and hung a four-foot canvas sign that read TO THE EGRESS.

Museumgoers coming down the stairs from the third floor stopped and read the sign, a replica of which appears below. Believing an egress was another exciting exhibit, they poured through the doorway—and found themselves outside on Ann Street. Only then did they realize that *egress* meant "exit."

IF BARNUM COULD NOT GET HIS HANDS on a genuine curiosity for his museum, he had no problem making one up. He often mislabeled displays, claiming that ordinary items were really historically important artifacts. Thus a wooden club was transformed into "the very one that killed the esteemed Captain Cook." A boat oar became "the very tool with which Miles Standish himself rowed his fellow pilgrims to our great American shores." And a deer antler became "a rare specimen of the horn of the mysteriously elusive unicorn."

PUTTING WORDS IN HIS MOUTH

"There's a sucker born every minute." It's a famous phrase—one that history has attributed to Barnum. But the truth is, he never said it. According to historian A. H. Saxon, the showman respected his audiences and would never have called them suckers. In fact, his philosophy was more along the lines of "there's a customer born every minute."

So if Barnum didn't say it, who did?

David Hannum, one of Barnum's competitors, uttered the words in frustration after crowds chose the showman's exhibit over his own. For unknown reasons, however, Hannum wasn't credited with the phrase. Instead, Barnum went down in history as the man who said, "There's a sucker born every minute."

When word began to spread that visitors to the museum couldn't always trust what they saw, Barnum didn't hang his head in shame. What, he asked, was wrong with "puffing up the truth"? Why couldn't he put a "coat of varnish on the hard facts of life"? Besides, he argued, people liked to be on the receiving end of a practical joke. They liked to be "humbugged." By a humbug, he meant something fake that is packaged and advertised so cleverly that people think it is real. "I don't believe in duping the public," he further explained. "All my humbugs are used as skyrockets. That is, they are used as advertisements to draw attraction to the museum. First I attract the people, and then I please them. Anyone humbugged by me gets their money's worth."

In those days, the idea of individual learning was sweeping the country. People were going beyond schoolbooks and classrooms to discover facts for themselves. They began evaluating information and debating topics. In both big cities and small towns, Americans began flocking to lectures on every possible subject. Wrote one French tourist, "In America, everything is lectured upon, from the history of mankind to the proper method of making pumpkin-pie." Catering to Americans' newfound passion for learning, newspapers and magazines started including articles such as "How to Render Soap from Olive Oil" and "The History of Whaling in New England." Publishers, meanwhile, began producing thousands of pamphlets on such diverse topics as "Birds of the Carolinas," "The Inner Workings of the Sewing Machine," and "The Geography of the Holy Land."

This delight in learning made it easy for Barnum to fool his audiences—and they seemed to enjoy it. By claiming that an article was scientifically or historically important, he drew the audience into his museum. Once there, most people happily debated whether or not the object was real. Even more exciting was the possibility of discovering how the prank was played. Explained one of the museum's ticket sellers, "First Mr. Barnum humbugs them, and then they pay to hear him tell how he did it."

In his diary, an English visitor to the museum recorded his own humbug experience. "'Is it real or is it a humbug?' I asked, and Mr. Barnum answered with a smile. 'That's just the question: people who pay their money at the door have the right to form their own opinions after they have got upstairs.'"

People did form their own opinions, and—humbugged or not—usually left happy.

As for Barnum, he earned a new nickname: the Prince of Humbugs.

THIS CARTOON FROM THE *NEW YORK HERALD* PORTRAYED BARNUM AS A "REAL HUMBUG."

Barnum's first big humbug was committed in 1842—"a pivotal year in my life," he later noted. Not only had he opened his museum that year, but in May, Charity had given birth to their third daughter, Frances Irena. Then in June, Barnum heard an amazing story from a Boston museum owner named Moses Kimball that would forever establish the showman's reputation for humbuggery.

Back in 1817, said Kimball, an American sea captain named Samuel Eades bought what he believed was the preserved body of a mermaid. The shriveled-up old carcass was almost three feet long. Above the waist, it had skinny arms and a humanlike head with black hair. Below the waist, it had the fin and tail of a fish. Captain Eades thought he could make a fortune exhibiting the mermaid. But he was wrong, and after an unsuccessful tour of Europe, Captain Eades died. All he left his family was a pile of debts—and the mermaid.

Eades's son sold the mermaid to Moses Kimball, who immediately got in touch with Barnum. "Wouldn't you like to exhibit *this* at your museum?" Kimball asked the showman.

Barnum certainly would. But first he asked a scientist to examine the mermaid. He wanted to know if it was real or a humbug.

"It can't be real," said the scientist.

"Why not?" asked Barnum.

"Because I don't believe in mermaids," replied the scientist.

Neither did Barnum, but he quickly decided that keeping an open mind could make him lots of money. "I'll believe in mermaids," declared Barnum, "and exhibit it."

But he couldn't just plop the mermaid out on display. He knew he needed to whet the public's curiosity. He needed to make his audiences eager and excited about seeing the exhibit. "Some extraordinary means must be resorted to," he decided.

So he began writing and sending fake reports to New York's newspapers. These fake reports told about a certain Dr. Griffin who was passing through America on his way home to England. In his travels, this "good doctor" had discovered many interesting specimens, including a "real-life mermaid," which he had caught off the coast of the Fejee (Fiji) Islands.

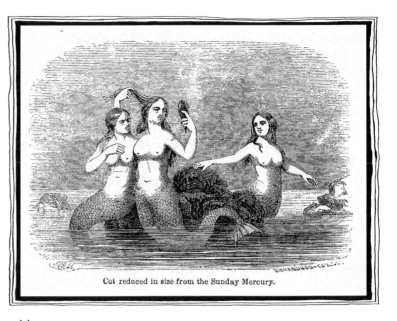

Cut reduced in size from the Sunday Mercury.

VISITORS EXPECTED TO SEE BEAUTIFUL MERMAIDS RISING FROM THE OCEAN, AS PORTRAYED IN THIS BARNUM AD.

Nobody knew that these reports had come from Barnum. Believing they were real, New York newspapers printed them. And their readers were instantly intrigued. A real-life mermaid? New Yorkers had to know more! With curiosity reaching fever pitch, Barnum sent one last report. Dr. Griffin, it said, would be stopping overnight in New York City.

In truth, Dr. Griffin was actually Barnum's old friend Levi Lyman, who had earlier helped with the Joice Heth exhibit. Using a phony British accent and wearing a pasted-on mustache, Lyman launched into a fake lecture about mermaids. Newspaper reporters ate it up. The next day, headlines proclaimed, "Mermaid Is World's Most Fascinating Discovery!!!"

Now New Yorkers were clamoring to see the mermaid for themselves. What else could Dr. Griffin do? He agreed to exhibit the creature for a week at Concert Hall. (Because Barnum's reputation for truthfulness was already in question, he did not want his name connected to the mermaid, so he decided to show it at Concert Hall first.) As "fish fever" grew, Barnum advertised endlessly in newspapers across the country. He had pamphlets and posters printed, showing a beautiful mermaid rising from a foamy ocean. He hung these all over town.

Finally, on August 8, 1842, the big day arrived. Thousands lined up to see the living beauty depicted in the posters. Instead, they were shocked to find an "ugly, dried up, black thing." Strangely, instead of hurting business, the ugly mermaid only helped it. Amateur scientists and mermaid believers alike jostled for a chance to get into the exhibit. Everyone wanted to see it for themselves and make up their own minds.

A week later, the mermaid exhibit was moved—where else but to the American Museum? For the next month, the "lady fish" remained on exhibit, almost tripling ticket sales. "I made money hand over fist," claimed Barnum.

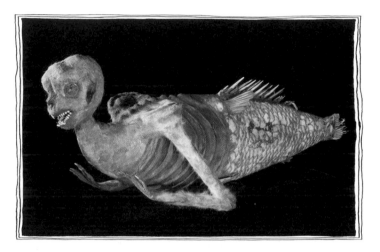

A MODERN-DAY PHOTOGRAPH OF THE FEJEE MERMAID SHOWS WHAT VISITORS REALLY SAW.

But not for long. Mermaids like Barnum's soon began turning up all over the world. They were, the showman learned, an example of a traditional Japanese art form. The mermaids were made by sewing the upper bodies of monkeys onto the lower bodies of fish. Red-faced, Barnum put his mermaid in a box and hid it on a high shelf in his private office. "The bubble," he wrote, "has burst."

THE WOOLY HORSE

Two years after the mermaid incident, Barnum bought a strange-looking horse from a traveling showman in Ohio. The horse was small and did not have a mane. Even stranger, it was covered with thick, curly hair that looked like sheep's wool. It was certainly a curiosity, but how to put it to good use?

An opportunity soon arose. That year, the famous explorer John C. Frémont had captured national attention when he had gotten lost deep in the snow-covered Rocky Mountains. For ten days, the public anxiously waited to learn if he had lived or died. Then, just as suddenly as Frémont had been lost, he was found—very much alive.

Barnum cleverly decided to play to this intense national interest. "The public appetite was craving for something from Colonel Frémont," he wrote. "They were absolutely famishing. They were ravenous. They would have swallowed anything, and like a good genius, I threw them a tidbit . . . and they swallowed it in a single gulp."

What was Barnum's tidbit? His horse, of course. Touting his wooly horse as the "astounding animal captured by Frémont near the River Gila," Barnum claimed it was part "elephant, deer, horse, buffalo, camel and sheep."

THIS ENGRAVING FROM BARNUM'S AUTOBIOGRAPHY SHOWS THE HERO JOHN C. FRÉMONT LASSOING THE "INCREDIBLE WOOLY HORSE."

Once again, New Yorkers poured into the museum.

But the exhibit soon caught the attention of the politically powerful Missouri senator Thomas Hart Benton. Benton was Frémont's father-in-law, and he declared the horse a fraud. "My son-in-law has never laid eyes on such a creature," he said.

Not wanting to tangle with the senator, Barnum quickly closed the exhibit and sent the horse to the country.

A GRAND BUFFALO HUNT

Not all of Barnum's humbugs were connected with the museum. Once, the showman tried to buy Niagara Falls—just the American side. His idea was to build a tall fence around it so people on the Canadian side would not be able to see it without paying an admission price. Needless to say, the scheme fell through.

TWO VIEWS OF BARNUM'S GRAND BUFFALO HUNT. THE TOP SHOWS AN IDEALIZED VERSION OF THE EVENT, WITH SAVAGE BUFFALO AND HEROIC NATIVE AMERICANS. THE BOTTOM SHOWS THE EVENT AS IT ACTUALLY WAS, WITH SCARED, SCRAWNY, AND VERY SMALL BUFFALO.

Another time, he considered lassoing a North Pole iceberg, then towing it by boat to New York harbor for exhibition. He decided the plan wouldn't work.

And when a sea serpent was supposedly sighted off the coast of Massachusetts, Barnum offered $20,000 to anyone who could deliver it to him. No one could, although a Tennessee man did write the showman, offering to catch a live wooly mammoth. "Do not be ridiculous," replied Barnum. "Everyone knows the great mammoth is extinct."

But Barnum's most famous humbug away from the museum took place in New Jersey after he had bought a scrawny herd of tame buffalo.

Barnum knew how much New Yorkers loved to escape to Hoboken, New Jersey, in the summer. It was cooler there, and easy to get to—just a ferry ride across the Hudson River. Barnum began advertising a "Grand Buffalo Hunt, free of charge," to take place in Hoboken in the hottest of all months—August. Portraying his animals as "dangerous beasts from New Mexico," he promised the public that the buffalo would be "kept behind strong fences to prevent possible injury."

Barnum knew that the most tantalizing word in this ad was *free*. What he didn't mention was the round-trip ferryboat fare of twelve cents that each person would have

THE PRINCE OF HUMBUG IS HUMBUGGED HIMSELF

People knew that Barnum was always on the lookout for new attractions and curiosities. One day in 1860, a farmer appeared in the showman's office with a squirming bag. In it, he said, was an amazing find—a cherry-colored cat. Barnum immediately paid the farmer twenty-five dollars, then opened the bag. Inside was an ordinary cat, and it was indeed the color of cherries—black cherries. Barnum thought the joke was so funny, he reenacted the "deal" in the museum theater. As for the cat, he joined the ranks of the Happy Family in the Seventh Grand Saloon.

to pay to get to Hoboken. Since Barnum had chartered all the boats that day, he would collect all the fares. "If it doesn't rain, I expect 16,000 people will ride that ferry," he gleefully wrote a friend. He anticipated a tidy profit.

The morning of the hunt dawned bright and sunny. Boat after boat made the crossing—some twenty-four thousand people in all. At exactly three o'clock, the skinny buffalo sauntered out of a shed in the middle of the fenced enclosure. Around them performers riding horses and dressed as Native Americans whooped and whirled lassos in the air. The buffalo were supposed to pound across the field as the fake Indians chased them. But the pitiful animals just huddled together and refused to move.

At this, the spectators howled with laughter. The noise coming from the crowd scared the buffalo even more. Breaking into a gallop, the animals burst through the flimsy fence and ran for cover in a nearby swamp. Meanwhile, the spectators—believing that the buffalo were stampeding—screeched with fear, then scattered pell-mell. Recalled Barnum with a laugh, "Such scampering I never saw!"

He made $3,400.

THE MAN IN MINIATURE

IN NOVEMBER 1842—less than a year after Barnum had opened the American Museum—his brother Philo told him about a tiny boy who lived in Bridgeport, Connecticut. The thirty-two-year-old showman immediately set out to see the child with his own eyes. The minute he walked into the home of Sherwood and Cynthia Stratton, he knew he had discovered a "gold mine." The Strattons' son, Charles, was the tiniest person he had ever seen. The boy barely came up to the showman's knees!

Little Charley, Mrs. Stratton told Barnum, had stopped growing when he was seven months old. Now four, he weighed only fifteen pounds and stood just twenty-five inches tall.

"He was a bright-eyed little fellow, with light hair and ruddy cheeks," Barnum recalled. At first Charley was afraid of the tall stranger, but once he started talking, Barnum found the boy "utterly charming." He immediately offered to hire Charley.

Mr. Stratton, a poor carpenter, was only too happy to rent out his little son for seven dollars a week, plus room and board and traveling expenses. Thus Charley and his parents were whisked off to New York City. Barnum gave the family an apartment on the top floor of the museum. He had elaborate little costumes made for Charley. And over the course of the next few weeks, Barnum taught the boy to strut and salute, to sing and dance. "[Charley] became very fond of me," admitted Barnum, "and I became sincerely attached to him."

Mrs. Stratton, meanwhile, had found an advertisement for her son's upcoming performance in a local newspaper. She was surprised to learn that Barnum was calling her son an eleven-year-old little person from England. Even more surprising, Charley had been given a new name: General Tom Thumb.

Why the changes?

Barnum explained: "If I had announced him as only four years of age, it would have been impossible to excite . . . the public. After all, aren't four year olds known to be small? As for the boy's birth, it is of no consequence where he was born or where he came from, but I had observed the American fancy for all things European and thought to profit by it."

And the name? It came from a story. The original Tom Thumb was a knight of King Arthur's round table—a knight so small, he rode a mouse and battled spiders. Barnum borrowed the name because he wanted to emphasize Charley's tininess.

General Tom Thumb took the museum stage and New York City by storm in January 1843. During his performances, he dressed up as famous historical figures like Napoleon and Frederick the Great. He danced, sang songs, and made jokes. Often, Barnum turned to the audience and asked for a little boy to volunteer to compare his size with Tom's. "I'd rather have a little miss," Tom would pipe up in his squeaky voice. The audience would howl with laughter.

LITTLE PEOPLE IN THE SPOTLIGHT

Tom Thumb was not the first midget to perform in public. Little people had appeared on the stage since the time of the Egyptian pharaohs, and European showmen had been exhibiting them for centuries. Henry VIII of England had a little person named Will Sommers as his court jester in the 1500s. And a Polish dwarf called Count Boruwlaski toured Europe during the 1700s, eventually becoming a favorite of the king of France. In America, midgets such as Calvin Phillips and Major Stevens became celebrities after traveling from town to town at the beginning of the nineteenth century. By Barnum's time, little people were common and popular performers.

So what made Tom such a sensation? Not only was he pert and smart, but he stayed tiny his entire life, never growing taller than twenty-five inches. "He was the perfect man-child, the perpetual boy," said Barnum. And audiences identified with him. "Anyone who had ever dreamed about never growing up fell in love with Tom Thumb," remembered one audience member. "They delighted in seeing one so small mock the mighty; adults also found irresistible the combination of innocence and pomposity."

Trained to speak and act like a man, Tom found that his career ended any sort of normal childhood he might have had. At five he learned to drink wine with his meals, and at seven he took up cigar smoking. "[I] never had any childhood, any boy-life," he once recalled. Still, he seemed to enjoy his stage career. Not only was he earning lots of money (Barnum increased his salary to $100 a week after the first month of performances), but he was famous, too.

Soon, Barnum decided to take his "man in miniature" to Europe. Leaving Charity and his daughters behind, the showman and his performer set sail in January 1844. They arrived in England eighteen days later. Not wanting anyone to get a glimpse of Tom before his show opened at the Egyptian Theatre, Barnum disguised the boy as a baby and carried him into the hotel.

Night after night, Londoners flocked to see the tiny boy. Then one night, the audience arrived to find a sign on the theater door. It read:

CLOSED THIS EVENING,
GENERAL TOM THUMB BEING AT BUCKINGHAM PALACE
BY COMMAND OF HER MAJESTY.

It was exactly what Barnum had been dreaming about since leaving New York City—a visit with Queen Victoria herself!

Little Tom wasn't sure how to behave around a queen. He addressed her as "ma'am" rather than "Your Majesty." He forgot his manners and licked his butter knife at the table. But the queen was not offended. Instead, she found Tom so delightful that eight days later she invited him back. Said Barnum, glowing, "If I was not such a modest man, I should probably brag a little, and say that I have done what no American ever before accomplished . . . visited the queen at her palace *twice* within eight days."

From England, Tom and Barnum traveled on to France. Paris went crazy over the boy. Composers wrote songs about him; street vendors sold likenesses of him. One playwright even wrote a play in which Tom popped out of a pie and slid through a line of chorus girls.

There were so many visits to royalty that Barnum had a special carriage built for Tom. Only eleven inches high, it was painted blue and lined with silk. Drawn by ponies only twenty-eight inches tall and driven by children dressed in livery, it caused a sensation wherever it went. "It killed the public dead," crowed Barnum. "It was the greatest hit in the universe."

For the next three years, Barnum spent more time in Europe than he did at home. The showman made occasional trips back to New York to check on his family and his business. But he never stayed long, even when his family needed him. In 1846, he left a hugely pregnant Charity to return to London and Tom's tour. Weeks later, with only her mother at her side, Charity gave birth to their fourth daughter, Pauline Taylor.

Meanwhile, the money from the tour poured in. By the time he returned to the United States, Tom was living the life of a rich and famous star. He and his parents built an unusual mansion in Bridgeport, Connecticut. All the doorknobs were low, and the place was filled with miniature furniture. Tom also bought horses. He hired servants. He even owned a yacht, which he learned to sail on the waters of Long Island Sound.

But something was still missing. Tom was, as he once admitted, lonely. As the years passed, Barnum introduced his friend to various little women. But Tom always claimed he was too busy performing to be interested in love. Then in 1862 Barnum heard of "an extraordinary small girl."

The small girl was Lavinia Warren Bump, a twenty-one-year-old beauty from Massachusetts who was only thirty-two inches tall (seven inches taller than Tom). As a child, she had a pair of portable steps her father had built her, which she pushed around the kitchen so she could reach the top shelves. Later, when she became a schoolteacher, her size allowed her to run around beneath her students' desks and pinch misbehaving pupils. She quickly abandoned the classroom, however, when Barnum offered her $100 a week to show herself at the American Museum. Fame and fortune waited. So did love.

TOM THUMB'S MINIATURE PICTURE GALLERY

LITTLE CHARLEY STRATTON SHOWN WITH HIS FATHER IN 1842, THE YEAR BARNUM DISCOVERED HIM.

SEVEN-YEAR-OLD TOM IN HIS TRAVELING CLOTHES.

BARNUM AND TOM POSED FOR THIS PICTURE TOGETHER JUST BEFORE SAILING OFF FOR EUROPE.

LAVINIA WARREN BUMP.

TOM AND LAVINIA'S WEDDING PICTURE. PHOTOGRAPHED WITH THEM ARE THE BEST MAN, COMMODORE NUTT, AND THE MAID OF HONOR, LAVINIA'S EVEN TINIER YOUNGER SISTER, MINNIE.

AN ADVERTISEMENT FOR TOM SHOWS HIM STANDING ON A CHAIR, SURROUNDED BY PICTURES OF ALL THE ROLES HE PERFORMED ONSTAGE.

ONE OF THE LAST PHOTOGRAPHS OF TOM.

Tom Thumb and Lavinia Warren were married on February 19, 1863, in New York City. Even though crowds clamored to attend this unusual event, Barnum gave the couple a dignified private wedding at Grace Episcopal Church. Afterward, a reception was held at the Metropolitan Hotel, where the bride and groom had to stand on a grand piano to greet their guests.

After the wedding, Tom and Lavinia left Barnum's museum and starred in their own shows all around the world. Although the three remained close friends, the showman and the tiny couple rarely worked together again. When Tom Thumb died of a stroke in 1883 at the age of forty-five, Barnum was devastated. "He was not just a good performer," said the showman, "he was a good friend."

THE SWEDISH NIGHTINGALE

They called her . . .

"Singer extraordinaire!"

"The toast of Europe!"

"The Swedish nightingale!"

Twenty-nine-year-old Jenny Lind had taken Europe by storm in the 1840s. Her soprano voice trilled and thrilled. "She doesn't just sing songs," exclaimed one listener, "she lives them— now sadness, now happiness, now love."

Barnum learned about the "Jenny Lind mania" that was sweeping across Europe from a cover story in the *New York Atlas.* Although he had never heard Jenny sing, the showman wanted to cash in on that mania. Could he, he wondered, sponsor the great musician on a tour of the United States?

JENNY LIND AS SHE WAS PORTRAYED TO THE PUBLIC.

This would be no humbug. Instead, he hoped to introduce ordinary Americans to good music—something they had few opportunities to hear. "I myself relished a higher grade of amusement than jugglers and albinos," Barnum said, "and I was a frequent attendant at the opera, first-class concerts, lectures and the like." With dreams of bringing highbrow music to the masses (and making a lot of money to boot), Barnum approached the diva. She agreed. "I have decided to go to America," she wrote a friend. "The offer from there was so brilliant." (Barnum offered her $1,000 per concert, as well as five percent of the ticket sales.)

But the showman soon learned that few Americans had ever heard of the singer. When he mentioned her name to a train conductor one day, the man replied, "Jenny Lind? Is she a dancer?"

A PHOTOGRAPH OF JENNY SHOWS
HOW SHE REALLY LOOKED.

His words, said Barnum, "were ice."

"Really," he thought, "if this is all a railroad conductor working the line between Philadelphia and New York knows about the greatest songstress in the world, I am cooked."

The showman knew there was only one thing to do: create a media frenzy.

To get the ball rolling, Barnum paid thirty reporters to write about Jenny in their newspapers. The stories focused less on her singing than on her personal life. She was reported to have a "beautiful spirit," to be unselfish and saintly. This, Barnum knew, was what ordinary Americans would find appealing. "She will be adored," he wrote, "even if she sang like a crow."

In reality, Jenny hated makeup and fancy costumes, instead appearing onstage in a simple white dress without even a touch of makeup. She said she sang for Jesus and felt it was her duty to use her God-given talent to help others—no matter that she disliked thanking people, could not stand sitting at the table after she had finished eating, cringed at too much attention, wished she weren't a celebrity, was wracked with headaches, and plugged her ears at night to "shut out the noises of the world."

Day after day, stories, pictures, and reviews of her European concerts appeared in American newspapers. Overnight, Jenny's name was on everyone's lips. And while people might not have been sure about what she sang, they desperately wanted to go to one of her shows. After all, didn't the notices say "to miss being in her audience would be like turning your back on a rare appearance of Halley's Comet"? Nobody wanted to do that! It was the beginning of "Lindomania."

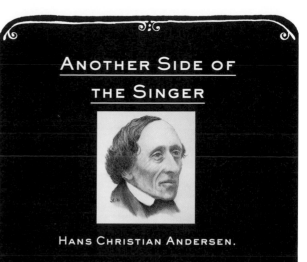

ANOTHER SIDE OF THE SINGER

HANS CHRISTIAN ANDERSEN.

Hans Christian Andersen, the great Danish writer, fell madly in love with Jenny in 1840, ten years before her tour of America. He wrote stories for and about her: "The Ugly Duckling" and "The Emperor's Nightingale." But Jenny could not have cared less. Once, Andersen traveled all the way from Copenhagen to London to be with her on Christmas Eve. But she left him alone and went out with her friends. When he begged her to tell him why she didn't love him, Jenny didn't say a word. She just handed him a mirror.

On September 1, 1850, Jenny's ship arrived in New York harbor. A mob of people—forty thousand in all—was waiting for her. Every wharf, window, and rooftop was crawling with people. They cheered, shouted, and tossed bouquets at the singer. The sight pleased Barnum. "They will take her to heart, and take out their wallets," he predicted.

He was right. Soon, requests for Jenny to sing poured in from all over the United States. A tour route was established, and Jenny and Barnum set off,

AN ENGRAVING OF JENNY'S FIRST, TRIUMPHANT PERFORMANCE AT NEW YORK CITY'S CASTLE GARDEN.

JENNY WINS OVER THE CUBAN AUDIENCE IN THIS ENGRAVING FROM BARNUM'S AUTOBIOGRAPHY.

traveling north, south, east, and west. Their route included concerts in:

New York City. The first concert took place on September 11, at Castle Garden, an auditorium at the Battery, on the southern tip of Manhattan, that held almost twice as many people as Barnum's museum theater. Five thousand people turned out to hear Jenny sing, and they were enthralled. "We were held in delighted and breathless suspense," said one theatergoer. By the concert's end, even Barnum was moved. When the audience called him to the stage, he said he wished to "sink into utter insignificance," so grand was Jenny's singing.

Havana, Cuba. Jenny arrived there in March 1851, and for the first time was booed and hissed by the audience. They weren't complaining about the quality of her singing, though. They were expressing their anger over the high price of the five-dollar tickets. Barnum was shocked—and worried. What if the crowd turned ugly? But Jenny summoned all her magic, and by the end of the evening the Cubans felt they'd gotten their money's worth. Exclaimed Barnum, "When I witnessed her triumph, I could not restrain the tears of joy that rolled down my cheeks. 'God bless you, Jenny, you have settled them,' I cried. And she, throwing her arms around my neck, cried with joy, too."

Memphis, Tennessee. Still just a backwoods town, Memphis didn't have a theater, so the city tried to "beautify" an old warehouse. The job still wasn't done when Jenny took the stage in April 1851. Holes in the walls let the wind whistle in, and people had to bring their own chairs. None of this mattered much to the audience, which was mostly men. They came wearing muddy boots and overalls and spat tobacco juice throughout most of the concert. Wrote Jenny in her diary, "They had obviously never attended a concert before, and expressed their appreciation by banging their chairs on the floor."

Eventually, all this traveling took its toll. Barnum grew tired of Jenny's temperamental quirks. And Jenny grew tired of Barnum's tight schedule. So

CELEBRITY!

In 1849, almost nobody in the United States knew who Jenny Lind was. By 1850, almost everybody did. With "Lindomania," Barnum created a new cultural phenomenon: celebrity. Newspapers that ran stories about or pictures of the singer sold out in hours. Enormous crowds turned out to greet her trains, ships, and carriages. Recognizing the public's hunger for anything Jenny, businessmen began making products that the singer put her name on—the first-ever celebrity-endorsed items. There were Jenny Lind beds, Jenny Lind pianos, Jenny Lind shawls, hats, cigars, poker chips, chewing gum, paper dolls, fishing flies, earrings, sewing machines, even mules' bridles! A glance at the ads found in the *New York Herald* on September 14, 1850, shows just how popular Jenny was:

> JENNY LIND PRODUCES PERFECT NOTES. BROOKS, OF 150 FULTON STREET, MAKES PERFECT BOOTS AND WHOEVER WILL MAKE HIM AN OVERTURE OF FOUR AND A HALF NOTES, CAN HAVE A PAIR. IS THIS NOT SELLING THEM FOR A SONG?

> OPERA GLASSES—A SUPERB LOT JUST RECEIVED AT TUTTLE'S EMPORIUM OF EUROPEAN FANCY GOODS . . . WORTHY OF THE ATTENTION OF ANY LADY WHO INTENDS TO GO TO THE JENNY LIND CONCERTS.

> JENNY LIND CONCERT HAT—A NEW ARTICLE FOR SALE BY JOHN & ROBERT OSBORN, 111 WALL STREET.

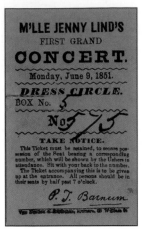

A TICKET STUB FROM ONE OF JENNY AND BARNUM'S CONCERTS.

even though the two had agreed to give a hundred fifty concerts across the country, they called it quits in July 1851, after just ninety-three. They had been on tour for ten months.

Jenny stayed in the United States for a while. She set up her own performance schedule, traveling as far as Biloxi, Mississippi, and San Francisco. But she never again received the public adoration she had with Barnum. After all, she later admitted, it was Barnum who had made her a star.

BARNUM HAD LOTS TO SAY ABOUT HIS MONEY, his museum, and himself. But he said very little about his wife, Charity. His round-the-clock work habits and long absences from home obviously took their toll on his marriage. In 1842—the year Barnum opened his museum—he complained to a friend that his wife was "nervous and given to hysterics," while he was "a good-natured guy who takes things easy."

But Barnum wasn't always good-natured when it came to his wife. At times, he was downright mean to her. Once, during a boat trip to Ontario, Canada, in 1843, Charity got seasick. Instead of being sympathetic, Barnum made fun of her in front of the other passengers. While Charity moaned miserably, he kept everyone else aboard "in a half-suffocation of concealed laughter" by telling her disgusting stories to make her feel even worse. That same year, when the couple visited Niagara Falls, they came upon 250 steep steps leading down to the river. Afraid of the staircase, Charity didn't want to climb down. But Barnum insisted. Halfway down, she got dizzy and couldn't go any farther. What did her husband do? He left her, of course. Later, he learned she had fainted. Two men had found her lying unconscious on the stairs and had carried her back to the top.

CHARITY, FIFTEEN YEARS INTO HER MARRIAGE, LOOKING MISERABLE.

Charity blamed her husband's bad behavior on his drinking, a problem that got worse while he was on tour in Europe with Tom Thumb. "Here, day after day, I reveled and ran riot among the thousands of acres of ripe, luscious wine grapes," the showman wrote. He toured dozens of vineyards, sampled endless bottles of wine, and shipped case after case home. "I have never been so happy in my life," he said.

Charity, meanwhile, was miserable. The more Barnum drank, the meaner he seemed to act toward her. In letters home, he called her a "sour old maid" and a "harping old millstone." His words stung. Often, Charity cried herself to sleep.

By the time he returned from Europe in 1846, Barnum was a heavy drinker. "I had gone so far in the miserable and ruinous habit of liquoring up that I could barely do business," he later wrote. Some days, he was drunk by noon.

Charity pleaded with her husband to stop drinking. But her pleading only pushed him away. By late 1847, Barnum was spending more time working than with his wife. Charity, he admitted to a friend, was "vexatious and annoying," and he was "not very happy" living with her.

Then one night, Barnum attended services at his Universalist church in Bridgeport. The speaker, Edwin Chapin, just happened to give a sermon in which he begged everyone in the congregation to give up drinking. "I warn you in light of all human experience, that you are in danger and should give it up for your sake," he preached.

Something in the clergyman's words touched Barnum. After a "wretched and sleepless night," he later wrote, he climbed out of bed and went downstairs to his wine cellar. There he "knocked the tops off of 60 or 70 bottles of champagne" and poured their contents onto the dirt floor. "I then called upon Mr. Chapin and took the teetotaler's pledge," vowing never to touch a drop of liquor again. It was the end of Barnum's drinking. When he went home and told Charity what he had done, she burst into tears. That day, he later admitted, "saved my marriage, as well as my life."

BARNUM'S DAUGHTERS, FROM LEFT TO RIGHT:
CAROLINE, PAULINE, AND HELEN. NO PICTURES OF
FRANCES EXIST.

"My daughters were brought up in luxury," Barnum once wrote, "accustomed to calling on servants to attend their every want; and with an almost unlimited expenditure of money." Little else, however, is known about them. While his autobiography is filled with anecdotes about actresses, singers, and friends, he wrote almost nothing about his children. Here's what we do know:

Caroline Cordelia Barnum was born on May 27, 1833, in the family's tiny apartment in Bethel, Connecticut. Her father, she once said, was like a shadow "flitting in and out" of her life. She longed for his attention but rarely got it. "Father was always busy with his miniature men and nightingales," she once complained. Still, as he grew richer, Barnum lavished clothes and toys on his oldest daughter. And when she was old enough, he took her along on some of his business trips.

Helen Maria Barnum was born on April 18, 1840, in the Barnums' tiny New York City apartment. Relatives always said Helen looked very much like her father. She also had her father's personality—she was "free-spirited and full of fun." Like Caroline, Helen rarely saw her father while she was growing up. "Father was constantly on the move," recalled Helen. Unlike Caroline, she never traveled with Barnum. "I did not really get close to him until I was a grown-up myself," she said.

Frances Irena Barnum was born in the family's ground-floor apartment at the American Museum on May 1, 1842. Barnum, who was in the middle of making plans for his Fejee Mermaid exhibit, gave the baby almost no attention. In February 1844, just weeks after he set sail for Europe with Tom Thumb, the toddler came down with a bad case of measles. She died weeks later. It took a month for the news to reach Barnum at his London hotel. Just days earlier, he had sent his little daughter several toys for her second birthday. Now, he wrote a friend, "a good and wise Providence has placed [her] beyond the reach of either pain or pleasure. I can work no more today."

Pauline Taylor Barnum was born on March 1, 1846, after her father had returned to Europe to oversee Tom Thumb's tour and search for new and unusual museum exhibits. Barnum did not hear the news of his daughter's birth until the end of April, when he arrived back in the United States. Hurrying home to the family's museum apartment, he swooped up the infant and held her close. Then, putting her back in her crib, he hurried away to his office to check ticket sales. "I always came second to show business," said Pauline.

By 1848, Barnum had made enough money to move his family out of its American Museum apartment and into a . . . PALACE!

He called it Iranistan, for its Middle Eastern style of architecture, and built it on seventeen acres in Fairfield, Connecticut. Modeled after the Royal Pavilion of King George IV (which Barnum had seen while in Europe with Tom Thumb), it was like a fairy-tale castle. One guest said that the mansion seemed to be made up of "a little Joice Heth, a sprinkling of Tom Thumb . . . the tail of an anaconda . . . and a slice of two fantastical giants . . . sprinkled all over with a magical powder."

Outside, there were domes and minarets soaring toward the sky. Inside, there were an octagonal greenhouse, a library done entirely in Asian land-scapes, elaborate stained-glass windows, and dozens of bedrooms. And on the top floor there was a grand ballroom. In its shiny wooden floor was written Barnum's motto: "Love God and be merry."

At Iranistan, he kept all kinds of pets: mandarin ducks, silver pheasants, a cow named Bessie who was allowed to nibble the plush grass directly beneath his bedroom window, and a pig named Prince Albert. But perhaps the most

IRANISTAN.

unusual animal at Iranistan was an unnamed bull elephant. On summer mornings, Barnum sent the elephant and his Asian-costumed trainer out to plow a plot of land beside the railroad tracks running toward New York City. Barnum hoped this unusual sight would surprise and delight the

BARNUM'S ELEPHANT PLOWS HIS FIELD AND GIVES RAILROAD PASSENGERS AN EYEFUL.

passengers so much that they would head straight for his museum.

A DAY IN HIS LIFE

In 1854, the showman gave a newspaper interview. It provided readers with a rare glimpse of his home life. His daily routine at Iranistan began before sunrise, he said. While sipping hot chocolate and munching on rolls, he made a "to do" list. Then, after a walk in the garden, he hurried to catch the train into the city. Once there, he took a cab to the museum, where he looked over accounts, spoke with his employees, and worked on his

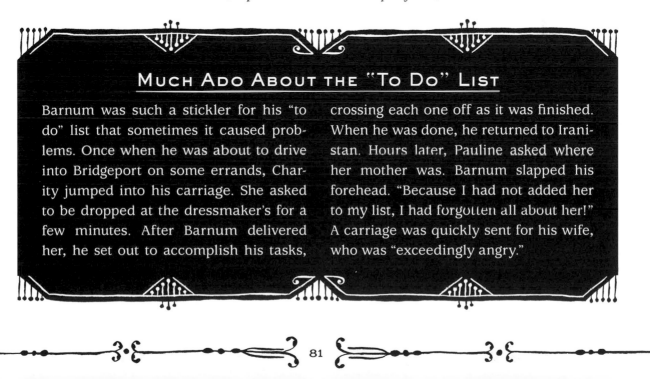

MUCH ADO ABOUT THE "TO DO" LIST

Barnum was such a stickler for his "to do" list that sometimes it caused problems. Once when he was about to drive into Bridgeport on some errands, Charity jumped into his carriage. She asked to be dropped at the dressmaker's for a few minutes. After Barnum delivered her, he set out to accomplish his tasks, crossing each one off as it was finished. When he was done, he returned to Iranistan. Hours later, Pauline asked where her mother was. Barnum slapped his forehead. "Because I had not added her to my list, I had forgotten all about her!" A carriage was quickly sent for his wife, who was "exceedingly angry."

newest advertisements. After finishing each task, he checked it off his list. Once everything was done, he caught the train home, where he napped after supper, then spent the evening reading in his library.

HIS WRITING

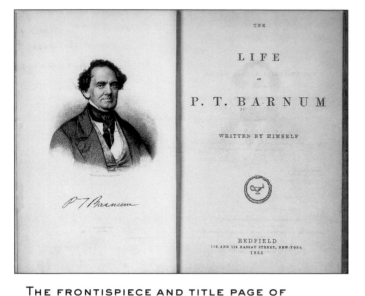

THE FRONTISPIECE AND TITLE PAGE OF BARNUM'S BESTSELLING AUTOBIOGRAPHY.

From his Iranistan library, Barnum also tried his hand at writing. In the summer of 1854, he began working on his autobiography— *The Life of P. T. Barnum, Written by Himself.* By this time, the showman was so famous that letters from as far away as New Zealand and addressed simply to "Mr. Barnum, America" found their way to his house. He knew he would sell lots of copies of his book.

More importantly, he wanted to leave behind a record of his life so he would be remembered as the world's greatest showman. The book became his "passion," and he tried to write out "what he thought and saw and dreamed and knew." In its pages, he told about his childhood and his rise to fame. He revealed the secrets behind the Fejee Mermaid and openly delighted in having humbugged so many people. It was, Barnum told a friend, his life's "monument."

When the book was published in December 1854, folks rushed to read it, just as Barnum had predicted. In the first twelve months alone, it sold more than 160,000 copies, making it a bestseller.

But not everyone admired it. "We have not read . . . a more trashy book than this," wrote a reviewer for *Blackwood's Edinburgh Magazine.* And the

Southern Quarterly Review called the book "the shameless confessions of a common imposter."

Barnum's feelings were hurt. Surely, he wrote, "there are some good streaks in me and my book."

CITY FRIENDS

Despite Iranistan's comforts, Barnum was a true city boy. New York, he said, "is the center of attractions in the way of operas, concerts, picture galleries, libraries, the best music, the best preaching, the best of everything." Because he loved the city so much, Barnum lived several months of every year there—first in a rented apartment and later in an elegant mansion on Fifth Avenue. (He had stopped living at the museum around the time he built Iranistan.)

Charity accompanied him until the 1850s, when she developed a mysterious illness that kept her in bed for weeks at a time. "When the hours of suffering were upon her," remembered one family friend, "the worst effect was on her nervous system." She grew fitful, worried, and sometimes so agitated that she had to be sedated. Unable to figure out what ailed her, doctors recommended rest and quiet. So Charity tucked herself into bed every night by seven p.m.

This left Barnum looking for ways to fill his evenings. He attended the theater. He went to the opera. And increasingly, he turned up at the home of the well-known poet sisters Phoebe and Alice Cary. Every Sunday night in their front parlor, some of the greatest minds of the nineteenth century gathered to talk, read aloud, or listen to music. Among the many visitors were the famous suffragists Susan B. Anthony and Elizabeth Cady Stanton; the gentle poet John Greenleaf Whittier; the influential editor of the *New York Tribune,* Horace Greeley; and the revered Norwegian violinist Ole Bull.

Barnum hit it off with these people. Wrote the lecturer and clergyman Charles Deems, the showman might have seemed an unlikely guest among

BARNUM'S FRIEND THE POET
PHOEBE CARY.

others of such literary and spiritual refinement, but he was their equal, "a man with great brains." The Carys' guests were drawn to Barnum's storytelling talents, his understanding of human nature, and his "burly good nature."

Phoebe Cary was especially taken with the showman. One night, when Barnum tried to leave early, she hurried into the front hall after him.

"Now why do you follow me out?" asked the showman. "I'm not going to carry anything away."

"I wish you would," replied Phoebe. And she flung open her arms invitingly.

The two grew closer and closer. Barnum took her for carriage rides in Central Park, invited her to dinner at his New York apartment, and shared with her hours of "rollicking laughter." He even gave her private museum tours. Once, while walking past the snake tank, Phoebe screamed and jumped back. Tripping, she fell into Barnum's outstretched arms. As he held her for a moment, she looked up at him and said, "Well, I am not the first woman who has fallen because of a serpent."

Charity knew of their friendship, but how she felt about it is anyone's guess. Still, Phoebe and Barnum remained close for almost twenty years, until Phoebe's death in 1871.

STILL A CHURCHGOING MAN

After building Iranistan, Barnum became the most influential member of Bridgeport's First Universalist Society. Not only did he give the church thousands of dollars each year, but he also paid for the organ, installed a new furnace, and covered the cost of repairing the steeple. Church ministers remembered how he stopped by the parsonage to "talk Universalism" with them or came by with a Thanksgiving turkey or some other gift. Every summer he threw a clambake on Long Island Sound for the whole congregation. And once in a while, he even preached from the pulpit. "His topics were surprising," remembered one churchgoer. He talked about the nature of the Gospel and of God's love. "[He] mentioned neither tigers nor elephants."

Barnum attended these church services by himself. Charity went to the Unitarian church (when she was well enough), and his daughters preferred the Episcopalian church—Bridgeport's most fashionable house of worship. But the showman didn't mind. He didn't think it mattered what church people worshipped in. "We may not all believe alike," he wrote, "but we can all be good."

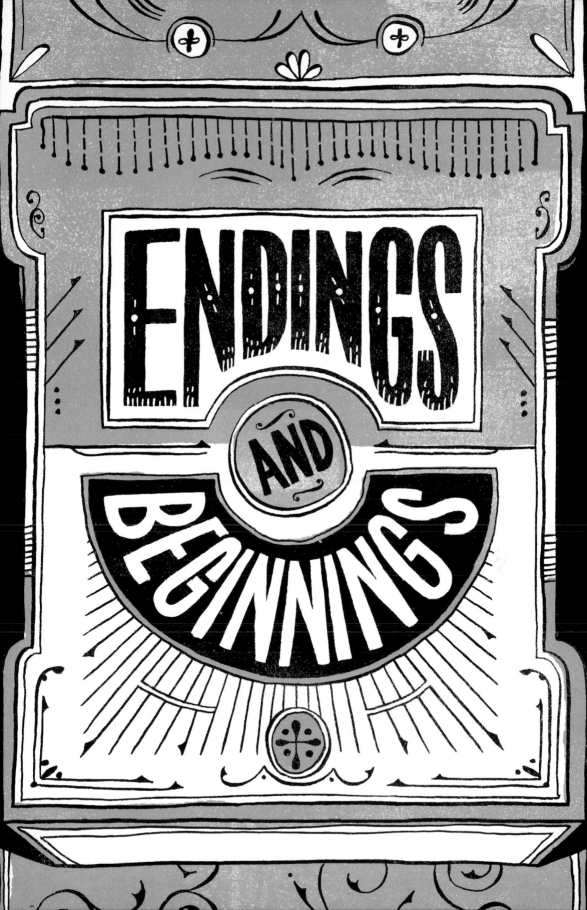

BANKRUPT!

IN 1854, BARNUM HAD A BIG IDEA: he would create a model town. Called East Bridgeport, it would be a place with cheerful streets and affordable homes; a place where citizens could work in clean, modern factories. The showman had no trouble finding people who wanted to live in such a town. The problem was, he couldn't attract any businesses to the area. And without businesses, people wouldn't have jobs. That was when he heard about the Jerome Clock Company.

The Jerome Clock Company was willing to move to East Bridgeport from Litchfield, Connecticut, but needed some financial help. Rather than loaning money, Barnum agreed to pay $110,000 of the company's existing debt. Over the next few months, he carelessly signed his name to dozens of notes on the clock company's behalf. Because he trusted the owners, Barnum never bothered to read what he was signing. Then one day in mid-January 1856, the "frightful fact" dawned on him. He had been tricked by the clock company's owners into assuming responsibility for close to half a million dollars of their debt! Creditors were now demanding payment.

Barnum didn't have that sort of cash lying around. Most of his fortune was invested in real estate—not just in East Bridgeport but in New York City, the city of Brooklyn, and many other parts of the country. Unable to pay what he owed, Barnum was forced to declare bankruptcy. "My impulsiveness and trusting nature has proved my ruin," he moaned.

Barnum's loss caused a national outpouring of sympathy. Complete strangers from as far away as Texas and Michigan offered the showman gifts and loans. The city of Bridgeport organized a "sympathy meeting," where citizens from all walks of life gathered to praise the showman and express their confidence in him. And *Frank Leslie's Illustrated Newspaper* ran a front-page article declaring its admiration for the "fortitude and composure with which [Mr. Barnum] has met reverses into which he has been dragged through no fault of his own."

Some people, however, rejoiced in Barnum's fall. "Here," wrote the *New York Herald,* "is a terrible illustration of where the practice of humbug must lead." And the *Chicago Tribune* gleefully declared in one of its headlines, "The deceiver is duped!"

As for the forty-five-year-old showman, his life changed almost overnight. In hopes of raising money, he put Iranistan up for sale and moved his family into a tiny rented house in New York City. He almost lost his beloved museum, too. But at the last minute, he managed to save the place by selling it for one dollar to his manager, John Greenwood. Greenwood promised to sell the museum back for the same price if Barnum could ever afford it.

"No man can comprehend the misery crowded into the last few months of my life," the showman wrote to a friend. Losing everything forced Barnum to take a look at his life, especially his "selfish pursuit of wealth." He came to believe that God was teaching him a lesson. Ever after, he saw the hand of God in every aspect of his life— good or bad. Everything that happened, he told himself, "has a purpose."

A PHOTOGRAPH OF BARNUM AT FORTY-FIVE, BANKRUPT.

THE ROAD BACK

One summer day in 1856, while Barnum was walking on the beach on Long Island, a dead whale washed ashore. The showman believed it was a sign from God—a new start. He quickly shipped the whale's carcass to the American Museum, where John Greenwood exhibited it for several days. Because it was Barnum's find, Greenwood sent the showman a share of the profits. It was Barnum's first step forward on the long road back to success.

Barnum took other steps, too. First, he negotiated with his creditors, convincing them to accept just twenty-five cents for every dollar he owed. Next, he lived as frugally as possible, even giving up smoking because his customary ten cigars a day cost too much. And finally, he began touring with Tom Thumb again.

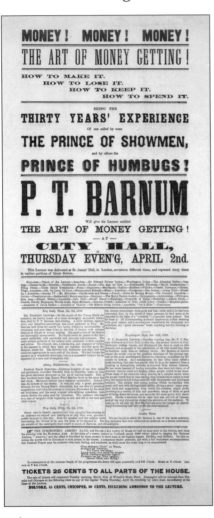

A BROADSIDE ADVERTISING BARNUM'S LECTURE "THE ART OF MONEY GETTING!"

"I understand your friends intend to get up some benefits for your family," Tom wrote Barnum when he heard the news. "Now just remember, my dear sir, that I belong to that mighty crowd and I must have a finger (or at least a 'thumb') in that pie. . . . I am ready to go to New York . . . and remain in your service as long as I, in my small way, can be useful."

Tom was indeed useful. That fall, the two friends once again toured Europe. It had been ten long years since their last trip. Still, they took the continent by storm. "We traveled from London to Berlin, performed for the crowned heads and crowded theaters, all the while making as much money as possible," recalled the showman.

But Tom wasn't a child anymore. Even though he was earning money for Barnum, he didn't need the showman to stay with him. So Barnum returned home and began touring the United States. For the next year, he spoke to audiences from Baltimore to New Orleans. He called his talk "The Art of Money Getting!" although he joked that lately he was better at "money losing." A funny and powerful speaker, he drew huge crowds and earned lots of money.

OLD HOUSES AND NEW HOMES

By the end of 1857, Barnum had made enough to move back to Iranistan, which he had never been able to sell. But the long-empty mansion needed some sprucing up. So Barnum sent in carpenters and painters. One of the workmen carelessly dropped a lit pipe. Within hours, the palace that had symbolized Barnum's success had gone up in smoke. "My beautiful Iranistan was gone," he said.

Was it a lesson from God?

Barnum believed so. Iranistan, he decided, was a symbol of the "old [gaudy] Barnum." But those days and that Barnum were gone. So in 1860, he built a new mansion.

It was nothing like Iranistan. While the old house had been the fanciful dream of a young man, the new house was a dignified manor. For the first time, the house became a family project. Charity, who loved growing flowers, designed the gardens. Pau-

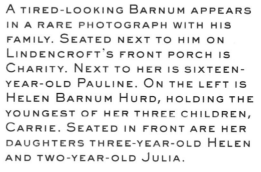

A TIRED-LOOKING BARNUM APPEARS IN A RARE PHOTOGRAPH WITH HIS FAMILY. SEATED NEXT TO HIM ON LINDENCROFT'S FRONT PORCH IS CHARITY. NEXT TO HER IS SIXTEEN-YEAR-OLD PAULINE. ON THE LEFT IS HELEN BARNUM HURD, HOLDING THE YOUNGEST OF HER THREE CHILDREN, CARRIE. SEATED IN FRONT ARE HER DAUGHTERS THREE-YEAR-OLD HELEN AND TWO-YEAR-OLD JULIA.

line, who was still a teenager, chose wallpaper and carpets. Even Caroline and Helen, who were now married and had their own children, gave suggestions. "My tribulations forced me to recognize how very much I adored my family," he wrote. Now he wanted a place to unwind; a place to talk with his wife; a place where his grandchildren could ramble. Calling the new house Lindencroft, he once again had a home.

WELCOME BACK

On the morning of March 17, 1860, P. T. Barnum bought back his American Museum for one dollar. That very afternoon, posters and banners appeared all over New York City. "BARNUM'S BACK ON HIS FEET!" they screamed.

A week later, the showman stepped onto the stage of the museum's lecture room. Cheers filled the packed theater, and the applause was so thunderous, it shook the building. In a voice trembling with emotion, Barnum said, "I have touched bottom at last, and here tonight I am happy to announce that I have waded ashore." Not yet ready to be "put in a glass case in

FABER'S TALKING MACHINE ASTOUNDED VISITORS BY SPEAKING IN THREE LANGUAGES WHILE THE LIPS AND EYES ON THE FACE MOVED AT THE SAME TIME. HOW DID IT WORK? BARNUM REFUSED TO GIVE UP THE SECRET. BUT HE DID HANG A SIGN ON THE MACHINE OFFERING $10,000 TO ANYONE WHO COULD FIGURE IT OUT. NO ONE EVER DID.

A POSTER ADVERTISING BARNUM'S CHICKEN CONTEST. AT ONE SUCH EVENT, EIGHT THOUSAND CHICKENS AND THEIR OWNERS GATHERED ON THE SECOND FLOOR OF THE MUSEUM. EACH OWNER HOPED HIS BIRD WOULD BE CHOSEN AS THE "MOST COMELY POULTRY." GASPED BARNUM, "GADS! WHAT A CROWING."

the museum as one of its millions of curiosities," he promised to make the place bigger and better than ever before.

And that was exactly what he did. Over the next few years, the museum exploded into new life with amazing exhibits, incredible performers, and sensational attractions. Onstage in the lecture hall there was Commodore Nutt, a twenty-nine-inch-tall man, as well as the Chiefs of the Nine [Indian] Nations, an exhibit of Native American leaders. Signor D'Olivera performed with his 200 trained white rats, and the Walby sisters enthralled audiences with their "dancing captivations."

There were puppet shows, a basement rifle range, a contest to find the handsomest chicken, Faber's Talking Machine, and the magic of Professor Anderson, "Great Wizard of the World."

Wrote the *Boston Saturday Evening Gazette,* "The old salt hasn't lost its savor."

A NEW CAREER: POLITICIAN

With his financial problems finally behind him, Barnum decided it was time to improve his public reputation. After all, many people still saw him as "nothing more than a professional humbug."

So in 1864, Barnum ran for the Connecticut state legislature. "I told myself that entering into the political arena would prove to one and all that I am filled with benevolence and public spirit," he wrote.

He was elected largely because of his wealth and fame. Many people thought Barnum wouldn't do anything valuable. But as always, the showman fooled them. He had strong, sometimes unpopular views, and he wasn't afraid to speak up. In his most famous political speech, he demanded that Connecticut's black citizens be allowed to vote. "A human soul is not to be trifled with," he declared. "It inhabits everyone, therefore everyone deserves equality under the law." His words fell on deaf ears. It would be five more years until African American men were allowed to vote.

Frank Leslie's Illustrated Newspaper published this engraving of the congressional candidate seated at his desk with a portrait of Jenny Lind on the wall over his shoulder. "In person Barnum is about 5 feet 10 inches and weighs 170 lbs," reported the paper. "He is always quick and energetic in his movements . . . and about his face there is a perpetual smile."

FIRE!

Meanwhile, another tragedy was about to befall Barnum. At noon on Thursday, July 13, 1865, museumgoers noticed smoke billowing past Old Bet, the stuffed elephant on the second floor. In those days, before building codes and fireproofing laws, the museum's wooden interiors and dusty exhibits were like a pile of old rags just waiting to ignite. Within minutes, the draperies on the first floor burst into flames; then the Cosmorama went up, and finally the main staircase. (The cause of the fire remains a mystery.) Because Barnum was not at the museum that day, his treasurer and son-in-law Samuel Hurd took charge. Shooing the approximately four hundred visitors out, Hurd ordered the water tank on the museum's top floor opened. Then, as blinding black smoke filled the place, he grabbed the cash out of the safe and made a dash for it.

Out on the street, chaos reigned. Thousands of spectators gathered to watch as firemen set up ladders, broke open windows, and began spraying water from their hand-pulled engines. One by one, the last people emerged from the building. Out came the museum's fat lady, assisted by Officer Dodge of the Broadway Fire Squad; next was Isaac Sprague, the Living Skeleton; and finally, Anna Swan, the giantess. Anna had been too big to fit through any of the available exits, but her fellow

THE AMERICAN MUSEUM BURNS.

performers had rescued her. They "procured a loft derrick from the Lecture Hall," reported the *New York Tribune*. "A portion of the wall was broken off on each side of the window, the strong tackle was got in readiness, [and] the tall woman was . . . swung over the people in the street and lowered to the ground amid enthusiastic applause."

Once all the people were out, the firefighters turned their attention to saving the animals. Barnum's birds were the luckiest. An employee had opened their cages as he fled, and parrots, hummingbirds, and vultures soared off into the New York sky. Ned the seal was rescued by a fireman, "pulled out by his flukes," reported the *New York Clipper*. The snakes, too, managed to save themselves, slithering through the crowd on the street. All the other animals—

the monkeys, lions, zebras, polar bears, and beluga whales—perished in the flames.

Two hours later, the outer walls of the museum collapsed. With everything lost, Hurd wired Barnum the terrible news.

Barnum received the news while speaking to the Connecticut legislature in Hartford. "I glanced over the dispatch, folded it, laid it on my desk, and calmly finished my speech as if nothing had happened," he later recalled. Then the showman, who had come to believe that everything (even the destruction of his museum) was God's will, ended his speech, drove home, and went to bed. Not until the next morning did he travel to New York to inspect the damage.

"I have lost an assemblage of rarities which half a million dollars cannot restore, and a quarter of a century cannot collect," moaned Barnum. At first he thought about retiring. "Accept this fire as a notice to quit and go a-fishing," he wrote. But quitting was not in Barnum's blood. Instead, he began planning a new museum.

WELCOME TO THE NEW AMERICAN MUSEUM

Six weeks later, Barnum opened his new American Museum just blocks from the ruins of his old place. "How did he manage it?" the *New York Times* marveled.

The truth was Barnum had worked like "a demon." After renting a three-story building on the corner of Broadway and Spring Street, he sent his agents scurrying across the world in search of "animal, vegetable and mineral curiosities." From London, he imported a collection of skins, tusks, heads, and skeletons of nearly every large African animal. He leased an exhibit of Chinese objects and figurines. And he formed a partnership with the world-famous animal trainer Isaac Van Amburgh, who brought his lions and tigers, zebras and camels, hyenas, kangaroos, ibexes, and polar bears to the museum. All the while, the showman used his inventive mind to fill every nook and cranny of the new building with the unusual and the un-expected.

The new museum quickly became as popular as the old one. Visitors could again see a menagerie of exotic animals. They could sit in the newly built lecture hall and watch clowns and acrobats. They could even wander through various rooms and again meet Barnum's bearded ladies, human skel-etons, and tiny men—many of them performers who had appeared at the old museum.

There were some new surprises, too. Barnum now presented an art gallery with paintings borrowed from local art museums. On the rooftop there was an ice cream parlor. And on the first floor he had a photography studio where customers could have their portraits made while they waited.

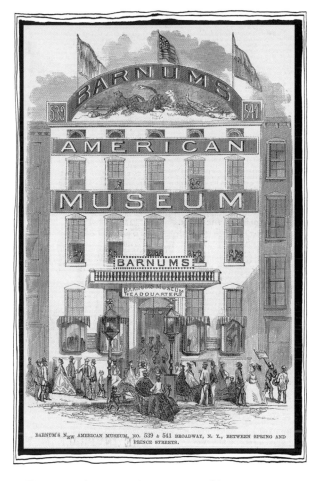

BARNUM'S NEW AMERICAN MUSEUM.

"It is," said one visitor, "a splendiferous place."

THE END OF A POLITICAL CAREER

During this time, Barnum continued working as a state legislator. In 1867, he decided to run for the United States Congress. But voters didn't think the showman was respectable enough for that job. "Can Connecticut find no one more fitting than the owner of the wooly horse and the bearded lady?" sneered the *New York Herald*. Unable to shake his humbug reputa-tion, Barnum lost the election by a landslide.

But he wasn't upset. He was tired, he wrote, of trying to be "all things to all men," of having to "shake hands with people I despise," and to "kiss the dirty babies of those whose votes counted." Happily, Barnum gave up the life of the "oily politician" and returned to the business of his museum.

But that business would be short-lived.

FIRE! FIRE!

On March 3, 1868, just after midnight, a fire—possibly caused by a spark in the boiler room—broke out in the new American Museum. The animals caught wind of it first, whimpering and howling and throwing themselves against the bars of their locked cages. Their screams woke the performers asleep in the apartments upstairs. After sounding the fire alarms, the show-people fled to a tavern across the street to wait for the fire engines.

They waited a long time. Because of thick snow on the roads, it took the fire engines almost an hour to get there. When they finally did arrive, the water from their hoses turned to ice. All they could do was watch the building burn. Within hours, flames had destroyed the museum and everything inside it.

HARPER'S WEEKLY CAPTURED THE HORRIBLE FATE
OF BARNUM'S ANIMALS IN THIS ENGRAVING.

"Those poor animals," Barnum moaned the next day. "Those poor animals."

This time it really was over. "I haven't the heart to start up again," said the showman.

WHAT'S NEXT?

For the next two years, Barnum did nothing but hang around Lindencroft. He played with his grandchildren and spent time with Charity. "I am retired," he said. "I have done work enough, and shall play the rest of my life."

With so much time on his hands, Barnum decided to build a new mansion, this one overlooking the ocean. As always, when

THE DAY AFTER THE FIRE, ONLY THE ICE-COVERED FRONT OF THE NEW AMERICAN MUSEUM WAS LEFT STANDING.

Barnum wanted something, he wanted it fast. Waldemere, as the house was named, was built in just eight months. Once it was completed, he turned his attention to building three more cottages on the property for his daughters and their families. But after those were built, Barnum didn't know what to do with himself. "I have lived so long on excitement, pepper and mustard that plain bread don't agree with me," he admitted to a friend.

By 1870, he was bored to tears. "Reading is merely pleasant for a while; writing without any special purpose soon tires; a game of chess is only occasionally entertaining; lectures, concerts, operas and dinner parties are well enough in their way; but to a healthy, robust man . . . something else is needed to satisfy."

GRANDPA BARNUM

Barnum was a grandpa nine times over, with six granddaughters and three grandsons. And he enjoyed their company in ways he had never enjoyed his daughters'. Now he had more time to take walks, make jokes, and go for pony rides. There was time to read "his dear babies" stories and teach them how to add long columns of numbers. (This last skill was especially important, because Barnum hoped his grandsons would follow in his footsteps and become businessmen.) Spending time with his grandchildren also made the showman think about children's education and training, a subject he'd never been interested in before. He believed parents should be taught to talk to their children in plain English and pronounce words correctly. "There's too much pootsy-tootsy, mamby-pamby baby talk," he said. Instead, a child's mind "should be sacredly respected." Above all, he felt a "child's sense of humor is the most important thing."

TAKEN DURING HIS RETIREMENT PERIOD, THIS IS THE ONLY KNOWN PHOTOGRAPH OF BARNUM WITH A BEARD. HE IS HOLDING ONE OF HIS GRANDDAUGHTERS, JESSIE.

But what?

As if in answer to a prayer, a letter arrived.

"Would the famous showman consider teaming up with my tiny circus?" asked the letter's writer, William C. Coup.

Would he ever!

At age sixty, P. T. Barnum was joining the circus.

BARNUM BUBBLED OVER WITH IDEAS FOR THE CIRCUS. Besides clowns and horse acts, the new partners could display mummies, Eskimo artifacts, wax figures! "We can make a stunning museum department," he excitedly wrote Coup.

Over the winter of 1870–71, the circus took shape. Barnum had been in show business a long time, and he knew whom to contact for extraordinary exhibits and acts. By April 1871, P. T. Barnum's Grand Traveling Museum, Menagerie, Caravan and Circus opened in Brooklyn, New York. (The partners had decided to use just Barnum's name because it was so famous.) In many ways, their entertainment was more like a museum on wheels than a circus. The first week, ten thousand people peered through the flickering gaslight that illuminated the dark corners of the big tent to see animals, artifacts, and Human Curiosities. Then the circus took to the road—the biggest of its kind ever to travel the country. One hundred wagons were needed: twenty of them for the museum collection alone, and at least ten for the wild animals. The wagon train also carried seventy-five full-time employees, sixty performers, and five acres of canvas tent. "It is the largest group of wonders ever known," proclaimed Barnum. "It totally eclipses all other exhibitions in the world!"

Barnum himself rarely traveled with the show. Instead, he remained in New York City, overseeing his financial empire, which included not only the circus but also his many real estate interests and other business dealings. Still, his favorite investment was the circus, and he visited whenever he could.

WILLIAM C. COUP, BARNUM'S FIRST CIRCUS PARTNER.

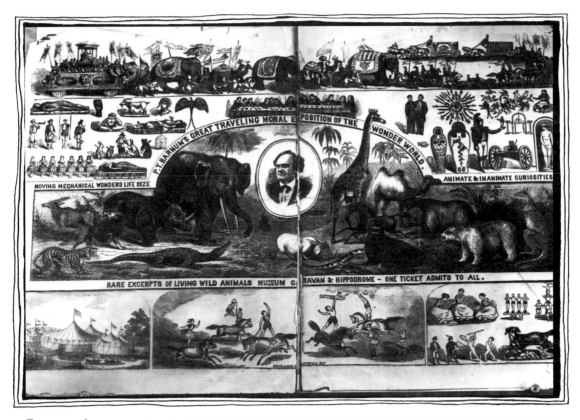

BARNUM'S EARLY CIRCUSES LOOKED MORE LIKE MUSEUMS ON WHEELS, AS THIS
AD PROVES.

He liked to sit in the stands and watch the show "like regular folk." Often, he took notes on how an act might be improved, then passed along
the suggestions to the performers. And he was always on the lookout for
what he called "indecent behavior." Barnum insisted his circus be a "moral
community"—a safe and comfortable place for families to visit. To this end,
he discouraged swearing among his employees, encouraged modest costumes, and prohibited drinking on the premises. "All of my employees are
teetotalers of gentlemanly behavior," he once noted.

Because Barnum didn't travel with the circus, he didn't oversee its day-to-
day operation. He didn't concern himself with the details of transporting,
setting up, or taking down the show, nor did he hire or fire any employees
except for performers. These responsibilities fell to Coup (and to later circus partners). Instead, Barnum contributed grand ideas, most of the investment money, and his name. Barnum's was a name that had been before the

public for more than thirty years—a guarantee in many people's minds of the strangest and most exciting, the best and the biggest.

It was the size of Barnum's circus that worried his new partner. "You are spending money like water," warned Coup.

But Barnum brushed his partner's fears aside. "We ought to have a big show," he replied. "The public expects it, and will appreciate it."

The public proved the showman right. In its first year, Barnum's big show made $40,000 (close to $5 million today). But Barnum figured he could earn even more if he made his show more efficient. Like other circuses of the time, Barnum's traveled by horse and wagon. But the roads were not paved, and every time it rained, they became so muddy that people couldn't travel on them. Over and over, Barnum's circus got bogged down in the mud. It could be days or even weeks late for a performance. And a late performance meant lost money.

THE HISTORY OF THE CIRCUS

While P. T. Barnum gave the circus its size, its wildest popularity, and its most memorable attractions, he did not invent it. The circus as a form of entertainment has been part of human history for thousands of years. There were circuses back in the ancient days of Egypt and Greece. Early Roman circuses featured animal duels and chariot races. But the circus as we know it was created by an Englishman named Philip Astley. In 1768, he gave his circus a riding ring and horse acts. Later, he added clowns, acrobats, a tightrope walker, and a three-piece band. Another Englishman, John Bill Ricketts, introduced this type of circus to the United States when his troupe performed in Philadelphia in 1793. President George Washington went to that show and enjoyed it so much, he went again the next night. By the time Barnum became interested in the circus some eighty years later, dozens of small traveling shows crisscrossed the country by horse and wagon. Pitching their tiny tents on the village green, they juggled and tumbled for a few dollars. Barnum would soon change all that.

So Barnum hit on the idea of using the railroad. Since the Civil War, the country had built twenty-six thousand miles of tracks, reaching into some of the nation's most remote areas. Barnum realized that if his show became a "railroad circus," it would not only move faster between larger cities, but it would also be able to perform in places that had once been considered too far away. It was a daring idea.

P. T. BARNUM'S GREAT SHOW.

M. H. PORTER, Photographer.   KALAMAZOO, MICH.

THIS RARE VIEW OF THE BARNUM SHOW WAS PHOTOGRAPHED FROM ATOP A FREIGHT CAR THE SEASON THE CIRCUS FIRST TOOK TO THE RAILROAD TRACKS. IT SHOWS THE LINEUP OF TENTS AND HOW CLOSE THEY WERE TO THE RAILS.

And it worried Coup. "It'll cost a fortune," he cried.

"It'll make a fortune," Barnum replied.

Barnum immediately had special circus cars built and within weeks was moving his show by railroad. Now it could travel a hundred miles in a single night (with horse and wagon, it had averaged only ten). After parading through a town early the next morning while the tent was being raised, the show could give two full performances in the afternoon and evening, then pack up and move on to the next stop in time to begin all over the following day. Barnum estimated they were giving three times as many performances—and making three times as much money.

That was when a new problem arose. Up to this time, circuses had featured a single center ring inside which all the acts had been performed. But Barnum's show had become too big for just one ring. His tent now seated twelve thousand people, and those sitting far back could not see the action. During the show, they either stood up or rushed to the front, pushing, jostling, and making other circusgoers angry. More than once, fistfights had broken out as spectators battled to see.

Barnum solved this problem by adding a second ring in 1873. This meant giving a double performance, but it also kept people in their seats. Circusgoers now stayed where they were, because they could see just as well from their part of the tent as from any other. The idea "hit the popular fancy," recalled Coup, "and within months smaller showmen all over the country began to give two-ring performances. Indeed, from that time it seemed to me that the old one-ring show was entirely forgotten."

The two-ring show would soon be forgotten as well. Recognizing its popularity, Barnum decided to go even bigger and add a third ring. And so America's three-ring circus was born!

A PHOTOGRAPH OF THE INTERIOR OF BARNUM'S CIRCUS AFTER IT WAS EXPANDED TO THREE RINGS.

LOSS AND LOVE

In September 1873, Barnum set sail for Europe in search of new acts and animals for the circus. Charity did not go with him. She rarely left her bedroom now, and doctors had recently diagnosed her as having heart disease. Still, Barnum didn't seem much concerned about her health. "The doctors say they think Mrs. B. will worry through, but are not *quite* sure," he wrote to a friend just weeks before his departure.

On November 20, while buying racing ostriches in Hamburg, Germany, the showman received a telegram. Charity was dead. Sadly, Barnum bowed his head and tried to imagine his wife's funeral taking place back home. Then he finalized the details of the ostrich deal and set sail for London. He longed, he wrote, to be with "sympathizing friends."

One of these was twenty-three-year-old Nancy Fish, daughter of one of Barnum's closest friends. She welcomed him into her home in Lancaster, England, and over the next few weeks, a love affair blossomed quickly. On Valentine's Day 1874, not quite thirteen weeks after Charity's death, Nancy and the sixty-three-year-old showman were married.

But they kept their happy news a secret. In April, the showman returned to the United States without his new bride and went about pretending to be the heartbroken widower. "I cannot enjoy things as I could before Mrs. Barnum died," he wrote to a friend just weeks after his wedding. "Still, time is helping me along . . . and eventually I should be alright." He did nothing to stifle rumors that he might someday marry one of Bridgeport's middle-aged women. "Instead I kept my own counsel," Barnum later wrote. "When I got ready, I brought home my English bride."

Nancy didn't arrive in the United States until September. Then the already married couple held another wedding ceremony for family and friends. Not a single guest knew that Barnum and Nancy were already husband and wife. And the couple never let anyone in on their secret. It wasn't until their marriage certificate was discovered 120 years later that the world learned that the two had truly been married in February, rather than September.

BARNUM POSES WITH HIS SECOND WIFE, NANCY FISH.

Why did they keep their marriage a secret? No one knows for sure, but historians have speculated that Barnum was concerned about his daughters' reaction. After all, his new wife was four years younger than his youngest daughter, Pauline. Would they accept Nancy as their stepmother? Obviously not. According to family accounts, when Barnum and his bride returned from honeymooning in Saratoga, New York, they found his family waiting on the front porch. They were all dressed in their best mourning clothes.

Barnum called his bride "my little wife" and was proud of having such a young English "girl" on his arm as they swept in and out of the best hotels, attended the opera, or sailed on the yachts of their wealthy friends. Intelligent, a gifted pianist, and a published writer, the second Mrs. Barnum intended to be a good wife. "Share his pleasure," she later advised other young brides in a magazine article. "Take your holidays together. . . . Don't spend your summers at the seashore, leaving him in the city; and don't stay at home in the autumn while he goes to Europe."

MAYOR BARNUM

A new business venture and a new wife weren't enough for the energetic showman. In the spring of 1875 he ran for mayor of Bridgeport and easily won. "All the beasts of the jungle roar their approval," the *Buffalo Express* wrote on Election Day, April 5.

Mayor Barnum got right to work. During his one-year term, he pushed to improve Bridgeport's water supply and worked to have gaslights installed on all major street corners. But he focused most of his attention on the Sunday liquor laws.

Like many other American cities at this time, Bridgeport had passed a law making it illegal to sell liquor on Sundays. No one, though, paid much attention to it. Instead, policemen looked the other way as citizens visited their local taverns after church. But Barnum, with his antidrinking sentiments, was appalled. "Laws are made to be obeyed," he said. He insisted that policemen begin arresting any tavern keepers caught selling liquor on Sunday and encouraged Bridgeport's citizens to report anyone seen entering or leaving a tavern. He would, he declared, "remove temptation from the paths of others, just as I have from myself."

But this strict enforcement did not sit well with many citizens. "Why can't I drink my beer in peace?" one man asked the city council. Others complained, too. So many groups came forward that the council eventually begged Barnum to loosen up on the liquor law. The mayor refused, and for the next ten months, he and his council feuded over the issue.

Used to getting things done and having his own way, Barnum found this job's endless compromises and delays frustrating. One year in office, he decided, was more than enough. So in January 1876, Barnum announced that he would not seek another term. A few months later, he turned all his attention back to the circus.

THE SHOW GOES ON

But things were not so happy under the big top. The partners had begun to squabble. Coup was tired of having Barnum making all the decisions. Barnum was tired of battling with his partner every time he had a big idea. So in 1875, Barnum bailed out of the partnership.

TWO ADS FOR BARNUM'S CIRCUSES.

He wasn't done with the circus, though. Over the next few years, Barnum went through several partners and launched several shows. His name blazed across the advertisements for each one:

"P. T. Barnum's Great Traveling Exposition and World's Fair."

"P. T. Barnum's New and Greatest Show on Earth."

"The P. T. Barnum Universal Exposition Company."

These shows were hugely successful. It seemed as if no one could rival Barnum. Then one day the great showman met his match. And it all began with a baby elephant.

By the late 1800s, elephants had become a much more common sight in the United States. Over the years, Barnum had kept dozens of elephants in his museum menageries, and when he joined with Coup, he bought several more. But no elephant had ever been born in America. Then in March 1880, Little Columbia arrived. Her birth in Philadelphia made big news for her owner, James Bailey of the Great London Circus. (Bailey's circus had this name even though it performed in the United

LITTLE COLUMBIA BESIDE HER MOTHER, HEBE.

States, not Europe.) Envious of all the publicity and eager to own Little Columbia himself, Barnum offered $100,000 for the baby elephant.

James Bailey refused. "Will not sell at any price," he wired back. Then he promptly used Barnum's offer in his ads. "Come see the beast Barnum himself would give a king's ransom for!" they exclaimed.

Instead of being angry, Barnum was impressed. "I have at last met [a] showman worthy of my steel," he admitted. Pleased to find someone whose business talent matched his own, he met Bailey "in a friendly council . . . and we decided to join our two shows into one mammoth combination." It was the beginning of the Barnum & Bailey circus (or sometimes Barnum and Bailey), as it was later officially called.

James Bailey would turn out to be the perfect partner. Squint-eyed and penny-pinching, he quietly took care of the details during the course of their ten-year partnership, while fun-loving Barnum took center stage. "You suit me exactly as a partner and friend," Barnum once declared.

FRIENDS AND PARTNERS: AN AD FOR P. T. BARNUM AND J. A. BAILEY'S CIRCUS.

ILLNESS

But Barnum almost didn't get a chance to enjoy his new partnership. On November 16, 1880, while he and Bailey were still ironing out the details of their first show, the seventy-seven-year-old showman suddenly doubled over in pain. Rushed to the hospital, he was diagnosed with a bowel obstruction. Unable to eat, he dropped from 215 pounds to 144. With his doctors expecting him to die, Barnum asked all the church congregations in Bridgeport to pray for him. They did. And the showman managed to hang on. Six long months later, he finally rose from his sickbed. But he was a changed man. "Old and stiff and not strong," he wrote to a friend, "I don't worry about business and never shall do so again."

PHOTOGRAPHS TAKEN BEFORE AND AFTER BARNUM'S ILLNESS
SHOW HOW QUICKLY HE AGED.

And so more and more of the circus business was placed in Bailey's capable hands. "A man my age cannot stand much worry or work," Barnum told his partner. "You manage it ten times better than I could."

While the showman recovered, Bailey set about combining their previously separate shows into one colossal circus. Now not only could visitors enjoy Barnum's traveling museum and menagerie—complete with Human Curiosities, Eygptian mummies, and even the original Fejee Mermaid—but they could also see Bailey's animal exhibits, his trapeze artists, and his troupe of clowns. Between the two of them, they owned twenty elephants, sixty circus wagons, "acres upon acres of tent canvas," and an assortment of exotic animals the likes of which had never been seen by most Americans. It was indeed, said Barnum, "the show of shows."

ABOUT MR. BAILEY

James Bailey always wore a derby hat to hide his baldness and had a dozen nervous mannerisms, such as twirling a silver dollar between his fingers and chewing on rubber bands. They were "dead giveaways that he was in a bad mood," recalled one circus hand, "and no one would go near him until he spat them from his mouth." But for all his strange habits, Bailey had a remarkable talent for organization. His methods for loading and unloading trains were so efficient, the U.S. Army sent a general to travel with the circus. The army wanted Bailey to teach the general how to move masses of men, animals, and equipment.

On March 16, 1881—with Barnum still in bed—New York City got its first look at Barnum & Bailey's big circus. As a mammoth torchlight parade made its way down Broadway, a half million people stood dazzled by the golden chariots and brightly painted wagons; the barred cages of leopards and hyenas and the glassed wagons of serpents; the 20 lumbering elephants, the 338 festooned horses, the 14 spitting camels, and the 70 costumed circus performers. As the magical procession swept endlessly on, four circus bands played rousing tunes, while a wheezing steam engine called a calliope puffed out a cacophony of musical notes.

The next night, the "Greatest Show on Earth" opened at Madison Square Garden, then on Twenty-sixth Street. Beneath the new electric lights (the first time they were ever used at a circus), nine thousand people gasped at the glittering display. For the next two hours, the three rings were filled with harnessed giraffes, bareback riders, tightrope walkers, dancing elephants, and much more. Declared the *New York Times* the next morning, "After last evening's spectacle, every man, woman and child begs to go to the circus."

Then the Greatest Show on Earth took to the rails. Over the next thirty-two weeks, it traveled from New York to Illinois to Texas. "Come One! Come All! To the Most Tremendous, Stupendous, Colossal of All Shows!" cried the advertisements. And people did. "Almost everywhere the circus went," said Barnum, "a crowd was sure to follow."

Barnum & Bailey's circus transformed—at least for a day or two—every place it visited. On an empty field on the outskirts of town, "canvas tents would pop up like mushrooms," recalled one circusgoer. Flags fluttered. Lions roared. The smell of sawdust mingled with animal manure and roasting peanuts, creating "an exotic ambrosia [that was] the very essence of the circus."

Barnum's "little city of canvas" spread across five acres. Beside the big top, workers called canvasmen labored to erect smaller tents for the sideshow and menagerie, as well as separate dressing room tents for the "lady and gent" performers, a cookhouse tent, an "eating saloon" tent, and dozens upon dozens of tents for sleeping and for stabling the horses.

The minute the circus rolled into town, the canvasmen set to work. Their calls "went on like a chant for hours," remembered one circus employee. "'Pull it, shake it, break it,' the foreman would holler, and the full weight of dozens of men would be thrown against the canvas. 'Again—pull it, shake it, break it.' And slowly, by pulling ropes and pushing poles and stretching

A RARE PHOTOGRAPH OF BARNUM & BAILEY'S "CANVAS CITY."

CANVASMEN STRETCH THE TENT AND READY THEMSELVES
TO PULL THE ROPES THAT WILL RAISE THE BIG TOP.

canvas, that big tent would rise. . . . [Then] the foreman would yell, 'Down-stake it!' And an eight-man sledge team would pound in the stakes at breakneck speed . . . the resulting noise was as regular as machine gun fire—smack, smack, smack, smack, smack."

It took hundreds of people (not including the performers) to get the circus up and running. Besides the 117 canvasmen, there were 19 trainmen who maintained the railcars; 17 ushers who helped audience members find their seats; 11 confectioners who made and sold many pounds of cotton candy every day; 7 ticket sellers; 2 laundrymen; a tailor; a shoemaker; and a watch repairer. On top of all this, the Hotel Barnum, as it was called, provided meals for circus workers. It was staffed by 10 cooks and 26 waiters. And there were animal trainers, veterinarians, blacksmiths, advertising men, ac-countants, printers, painters, and machinery repairmen. The "canvas city" even had its own postmaster. "We were a world unto ourselves," said one ticket seller.

A FOREMAN (FAR LEFT) BARKS OUT ORDERS TO A SLEDGE TEAM, WHO POUND THE STAKES OF THE CIRCUS TENTS INTO THE GROUND.

A BARNUM & BAILEY CIRCUS PARADE ROLLING THROUGH SOUTH BEND, INDIANA.

Once the tents were erected, it was time for the circus parade. Held before the first show, the parade gave "towners" a glimpse of the amazing events that would unfold under the big top. Ornately carved wagons pulled by plumed horses or zebras rolled down the main street. From these wagons, elaborately costumed performers waved, while lions yawned and bears panted in the heat. Behind them lumbered a train of elephants marching tail to trunk, and clowns ran alongside, passing out handbills to the crowd. At the end of the parade wheezed one of the circus's four noisy steam calliopes, inviting one and all to the circus. "It worked just like the Pied Piper," remembered one circusgoer. "Spellbound, we followed that parade right out onto the circus grounds."

Once there, visitors were met by the ticket seller.

"Step up! Step up!" he cried.

The price of a ticket varied. Folks who wanted to sit close to the action paid a whopping ten dollars, while others paid just twenty-five cents for a bleacher seat high in the stands. But no matter where a person sat, he could see all three rings. "The view was smaller," explained one ticket seller, "but it wasn't obstructed. Mr. Barnum

THIS PHOTOGRAPH OF THE BARNUM & BAILEY TICKET OFFICE SHOWS ONE OF THE SIDESHOW PERFORMERS (HOLDING A SNAKE) TRYING TO ENTICE THE AUDIENCE INSIDE.

made sure of that. He wanted everybody—rich and poor alike—to come to the circus . . . [and] he wanted them all to get good value."

With tickets in hand, visitors were free to wander the midway before the performance. Some stopped at one of the "grab joints"—refreshment stands lining the midway—for a paper cone of cotton candy or a glass of pink lemonade. Others bought one of the circus programs being peddled at the souvenir booth. Most, however, headed for the sideshow tent.

Set off from the rest of the circus, the sideshow tent had an allure all its own. (It was also an additional moneymaker.) "Come inside! Come inside!" the talker yelled as a tattooed man gave the crowd a peek at his colorful chest or a trained chicken plucked out a tune on a toy piano. "We have the fattest woman and the tallest man. Have you ever seen an elastic man? Or a woman who can charm snakes? The good Lord made them, so come in and see them—the Representatives of the Wonderful!"

After digging another dime from their pockets, circusgoers stepped into the tent's shadowy darkness. Over the years, the Barnum & Bailey circus employed hundreds of sideshow performers. Among them were:

Charles Tripp, an armless man who amazed audiences by doing with his feet what others did with their hands: painting a portrait, hammering nails, writing a poem, even serving a cup of tea.

English Jack, the frog swallower, who made onlookers gasp and gag by gulping down his wiggling meal. Once the audience moved on, however, Jack always regurgitated the frog, which was, according to all accounts, stunned but unhurt.

Captain George Costentenus, who was covered head to toe with tattoos—388 designs in all. While the captain claimed he had been tattooed by the Shah of Persia as punishment for falling in love with the shah's daughter, the truth was that the captain had tattooed himself.

Jo Jo, the dog-faced boy, whose real name was Fedor Jeftichew. Jo Jo, who came from Russia, suffered from hypertrichosis, or excessive hair growth. Even though he spoke three languages fluently, he liked to excite spectators by barking and growling at them.

Lucia Zarate, who may have been the littlest adult ever to have lived—she stood just twenty inches tall and weighed a mere five pounds.

The Seven Sutherland Sisters, who claimed to have the longest hair on record—"each with over seven feet of luxuriant mane." While the audience watched, the sisters tossed and swished their hair and sang songs. They also sold their "specially patented hair grower and scalp cleaner" during their performance.

Besides the sideshow tent, people could also visit the menagerie tent. Admission was free, and the place was usually crowded. One visitor recalled seeing "big cats and bears lounging in cages; llamas and giraffes fidgeting nearby."

When the lively strains of a brass band were heard, the milling customers knew it was almost time for the show to start. Following the

CHARLES TRIPP.

ENGLISH JACK.

CAPTAIN COSTENTENUS,
THE GREEK ALBANIAN
TATTOOED FROM HEAD TO FOOT
IN CHINESE TARTARY, AS PUNISHMENT FOR ENGAGING IN REBELLION AGAINST THE KING.

CAPTAIN GEORGE
COSTENTENUS.

Jo Jo' the Russian Dog-faced Boy,

Jo Jo, THE DOG-
FACED BOY.

LUCIA ZARATE.

THE SEVEN SUTHERLAND
SISTERS.

crush, visitors found their seats under the massive big top. Some of them might never have seen that many people in one place before; the tent had seating for twenty thousand. "A great sea of faces stretched out in every direction, representing all the county thirty miles around," remembered one audience member.

At exactly quarter past one, the time when all Barnum & Bailey afternoon performances began, there was another blast from the band.

Then the tent lights snapped off.

A spotlight snapped on.

The ringmaster stepped into the center ring. "Ladies and gentlemen, children of all ages, meet the most remarkable performers in the universe!"

Then—

"Prancing horses, tumbling clowns, bejeweled camels, elephants swaying to and fro, men and women in tights and spangles and breastplates of shining gold and steel paraded around and around in a heart pounding display

CIRCUS TALK

Circus workers used a language all their own, words and phrases only folks in the big-top business knew. Below is a sampling of their lingo:

Ballyhoo—The free show given outside the sideshow tent. For just a few minutes, sword swallowers gulped flaming swords, and belly dancers jiggled their hips in an attempt to enthrall audiences and sell tickets.

Beef—A complaint from a customer.

Blankaroo—A date on the calendar when no shows were scheduled.

Blowoff—The crowds leaving the big top after a performance.

Canvasmen—The men who put up and took down the big top as well as the smaller circus tents.

Gazoony—A new circus employee.

Geek—A performer who worked with frogs or snakes. English Jack was one.

Grab joint—A snack concession.

Midway—The area of the circus lot where all the concessions, souvenir booths, and sideshow tents were placed.

Pitch—A presentation during which a circus employee sold merchandise by lecturing and demonstrating.

Professor—Any performer considered an expert in his or her field. Among the many "professors" at the circus were "professors" of magic, "professors" of animal training, and even "professors" of stilt walking.

Punk—A child.

Roustabouts—The men who did the physical labor at the circus, especially the crew who set up the interior of the big top—the benches, chairs, nets, trapeze equipment, etc.

Talker—A circus employee who "talked" in front of an attraction. If he "talked" inside the attraction, he was called a lecturer.

Trouper—A person who had spent at least one full season with the circus.

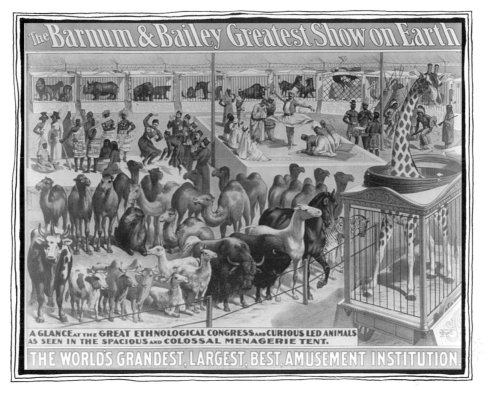

A POSTER ILLUSTRATES THE MANY ANIMALS FOUND IN THE CIRCUS MENAGERIE.

of pageantry," recalled an audience member. "The magical beauty of it all brought tears to my eyes."

Some circusgoers were lucky enough to attend a performance in which P. T. Barnum himself took part. During the opening act, the showman's specially built gold carriage would roll out. As it made its way around the tent's interior, it stopped every few minutes. Leaning out the window, the showman would shout, "You came to see Barnum? Well, I'm Barnum."

Sadly, age and illness kept him at home most of the time. Still, the old showman knew he was as much a main attraction as his acrobats and jugglers. Whenever he could, Barnum liked to "hit" the circus, as he put it.

When Barnum's carriage finally rolled back into the wings, the ringmaster would again step into the spotlight. "Cast your eyes to the center ring," he would direct the audience, "and be prepared to be amazed."

THE CHILDREN'S FRIEND

Barnum wanted his circus to make children happy. "A happy smile on a child's face acted like a tonic on the old man," recalled his son-in-law Samuel Hurd. Now when Barnum traveled with his circus, reported the *New York Sun,* he didn't watch the acts. Instead, "he waits for the children to tell him what they think of his great show." Barnum himself always claimed there was "no picture so beautiful as ten thousand smiling, bright-eyed, happy children; no music so sweet as their clear-ringing laughter." There is a story, which may or may not be true, about Barnum's love for children. When his circus arrived in Cleveland, Ohio, he heard about a little boy who longed to see the circus but was seriously ill and confined to his bed. According to the story, the showman changed the route of that morning's circus parade so it would pass by the sick boy's house. He even had some of the animals do tricks in the boy's backyard. His love of children was so well known that in later years people started calling him by a new nickname: the Children's Friend.

AN ENGRAVING FROM
HARPER'S WEEKLY
PORTRAYING BARNUM AS
THE CHILDREN'S FRIEND.

Here is just a sampling of the many stupendous acts that appeared beneath Barnum & Bailey's big top:

Shot from a cannon, Zazel, the "beautiful human cannonball," soared in an arc eighty feet above the audience before catching a trapeze bar.

Salamander, the Fire Horse, leaped heroically through a series of burning rings.

Karl Hagenbeck faced fierce lions and tigers with just a whip and a chair and made them purr like kittens.

And then there was the one, the only—

JUMBO!

SALAMANDER, THE FIRE
HORSE.

KARL HAGENBECK AND
HIS BIG CATS.

ZAZEL, THE HUMAN CANNONBALL.

In 1861, a baby elephant—captured in the African jungle—was sold to a Paris zoo. Zookeepers there waited eagerly for the little elephant to grow. They dreamed of an exhibit built around a gargantuan pachyderm. But the baby was sickly and didn't grow. Disappointed, the Paris zookeepers swapped their puny elephant for a rhinoceros from the Royal Zoological Gardens in London.

Named Jumbo by his new British owners, the little elephant was entrusted to the care of Matthew Scott. Scott, the zoo's elephant keeper, quickly bonded with Jumbo. He coddled him, scratched behind his ears, and fed him two hundred pounds of hay, fifteen loaves of bread, two barrels of oats, one barrel of potatoes, an assortment of onions and fruits, and five pails of water every day!

"Jummie is a big baby," Scott once said about the elephant. "If I am [late] he cries and whines and becomes very naughty, just the same as a child crying after its mother."

JUMBO, BEING FED BY A LONDON POLICEMAN.

Under Scott's loving care, Jumbo grew.

And grew.

And grew.

BARNUM VS. BERGH

Henry Bergh, a crusader for the humane treatment of animals and the founder and first president of the Society for the Prevention of Cruelty to Animals, heard about the act that featured Salamander, the Fire Horse. He ordered it stopped immediately. It was barbaric to "torture an animal that way," he declared. Barnum tried to explain that the fire rings that Salamander leaped through were not real. They were made with harmless liquid chemicals that gave off no heat. But Bergh refused to listen. So Barnum announced a special performance. Instead of Salamander jumping through the hoops, the showman would do it—just to prove that the act was safe. "Barnum vaulted about with admirable agility," a newspaper reported the next day.

Bergh was forced to admit he'd made a mistake. Still, Barnum knew that Bergh meant well. And even though the animal activist and the showman continued to lock horns over the treatment of animals, Barnum eventually admitted that Bergh should be "honored and respected for his unselfish devotion to such an excellent cause."

As for Bergh, he came to realize that Barnum would never knowingly mistreat an animal. He even recommended that the showman serve on the SPCA board because of his "generous and sympathetic instincts toward animals." Barnum soon became an active member of the society, and when he died, he not only willed a large sum of money to the SPCA but also left $1,000 to the city of Bridgeport to erect a statue in honor of his "dear friend, Henry Bergh."

HENRY BERGH.

By 1881, he weighed six and a half tons and stood eleven and a half feet tall—the largest elephant in captivity at the time.

He was also the most popular attraction at the zoo. A gentle animal, he happily swung his trunk as he sauntered across the shaded lawns. Children tossed him sweet rolls and oranges. People destined to become famous, like Theodore Roosevelt (age twenty-three) and Winston Churchill (age seven), visited him. Even Queen Victoria took a ride on his back.

Barnum also visited Jumbo. "I often looked wistfully on [him], but with no hope of ever getting possession of him. . . . I did not suppose he would ever be sold." But Barnum was wrong. In 1882—on a whim—he offered the London zoo $10,000 for the elephant. To his surprise, the zoo accepted.

British citizens were outraged. A movement to save Jumbo spread across London. Schoolchildren wrote to Barnum, begging him to leave the elephant in England, as did both the Prince of Wales and Queen Victoria. When Barnum refused, protestors drew cartoons, made speeches, and wrote editorials. Mourned the *London Daily Telegraph,* "No more quiet garden strolls. . . . Our amiable monster must dwell in a tent, take part in the routine of a circus, and instead of his by-gone friendly trots with British girls and boys . . . must amuse a Yankee mob and put up with peanuts and waffles."

Jumbo didn't seem to want to leave London either. On the day he was scheduled to depart, he stepped from the garden, trumpeted his unhappiness, and flung himself down on the pavement.

"Jumbo has laid down in the street, and won't get up!" Barnum's manager cabled the showman in New York. "What shall we do?"

"Let him lie there a week if he wants," replied Barnum. "It is the best advertisement in the world."

And it was. Excitement over the elephant grew in the United States as newspapers reported daily on Jumbo's refusal to move. Overnight, "Jumbomania" struck America. Merchants began making Jumbo hats, Jumbo neckties, Jumbo earrings, bracelets, cigars, and fans.

Finally, eight days after lying down, Jumbo rose and stepped into the specially made crate that would be his home until he reached America. "Jumbo is mine," Barnum gleefully declared. He eagerly waited for his newest attraction to arrive in New York.

Jumbo's ship reached America's shore on April 9, 1882. Thousands of New Yorkers waited at the dock, then followed the procession through packed and cheering crowds to Madison Square Garden, where the circus was about to open. Billed as the Towering Monarch of His Mighty Race, Jumbo was exhibited at every performance. Ticket sales soared, and Barnum credited Jumbo. He brought in $300,000 in his first ten days, $1.5 million in his first year. "I love that creature," gushed Barnum.

JUMBO ARRIVES IN NEW YORK CITY. IT TOOK TEN CIRCUS HORSES PULLING AND SEVERAL ELEPHANTS PUSHING TO ROLL JUMBO UP BROADWAY TO HIS FIRST PERFORMANCE AT MADISON SQUARE GARDEN.

As for Jumbo, he seemed to enjoy circus life. He marched in step with Barnum's four brass bands, gave rides to an estimated one million children, and gulped down endless peanuts and candy. While the other animals performed in acts, he didn't do any tricks. His size was what drew crowds. To make him look even bigger, he was regularly displayed beside a baby elephant named Tom Thumb. "Jummie had a real soft spot for that little one," recalled Matthew Scott, who had come to the United States with Jumbo.

Meanwhile, the word *jumbo* made its way into the English language. People began using the word when they meant big—really big!

Jumbo toured North America for four spectacular seasons. Then, on the night of September 15, 1885, Jumbo and Tom Thumb were ambling toward their railroad car when suddenly an unscheduled freight train rounded the bend. What happened next is anyone's guess. Some reports claimed that Jumbo charged the train headfirst. Others told how Jumbo shoved both Matthew Scott and the smaller elephant out of the train's path. Either way, it was Jumbo alone who took the train's hit.

CIRCUS FOLK POSE WITH JUMBO'S BODY JUST HOURS AFTER THE ACCIDENT. AT THE ELEPHANT'S HEAD STANDS A DISTRAUGHT MATTHEW SCOTT.

Matthew Scott raced to his side. Recalled one eyewitness, "The animal . . . reached out his long trunk, wrapped it around the trainer, and drew him down to where his majestic head lay blood stained in the cinders. Scotty cried like a baby. Five minutes later, they lifted him from the lifeless body of his huge friend."

Barnum claimed he was heartbroken, too. But since he never let sentimentality interfere with business, he immediately sent a pack of taxidermists to the site of the accident. His museums had once been full of stuffed birds and animals. Why not stuff Jumbo? "Lose no time in saving his skin and skeleton," advised the showman.

When the circus opened for the 1886 season, it had a new and gruesome exhibit: the "double Jumbo." Circusgoers would see not only Jumbo's skeleton, but also his skin, stretched over a wood frame. In the grand parade, the "double Jumbo" was placed on a wagon followed by a long line of the circus's regular elephants. The elephants had been trained to carry gigantic black-bordered handkerchiefs with their trunks and to stop every few steps to wipe their eyes. It was a season-long funeral for Jumbo.

The circus displayed the "double Jumbo" for the next two years. Then Barnum donated the skeleton to the American Museum of Natural History

THE DOUBLE JUMBO.

in New York City, where it is still periodically displayed. As for Jumbo's hide, that went to the showman's pet project, the Barnum Museum at Tufts University in Medford, Massachusetts. He had founded the museum a few years earlier after the Universalist Church established Tufts as its first college. Becoming one of its earliest benefactors, Barnum donated hundreds of specimens, artifacts, and collections. Now he added Jumbo to the list.

The stuffed Jumbo became the university's mascot. Even today, Tufts's sports teams are called the Jumbos. But in 1975, the Barnum Museum burned to the ground, destroying the hide. Only Jumbo's tail remains, tucked away in the archives.

THE CIRCUS AT REST

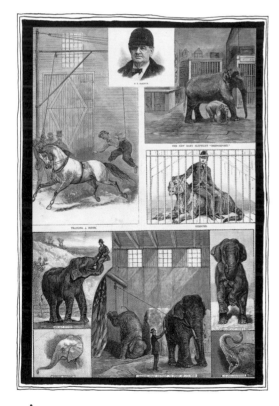

AN ARTICLE PUBLISHED IN *HARPER'S WEEKLY* ON FEBRUARY 18, 1882, SHOWS ACTIVITIES AT THE CIRCUS'S WINTER QUARTERS.

Barnum & Bailey's circus didn't perform during the cold months, so it needed a place where the animals could rest and the employees could repair their equipment and practice their acts. After some thought, the partners agreed to build winter quarters on five acres of Barnum's own property in Bridgeport, Connecticut. "I will awaken each morning to the trumpet of elephants and the smell of sawdust," he merrily told a friend.

The men spared no expense in building the place. By the mid-1880s, the winter quarters were the largest animal-training ground in the world. Steam heated, they had special housing for hippos, sea lions, monkeys, giraffes, big cats, and elephants. There was a main building big enough for dozens of elephants, and another with regulation-size rings for human performers to practice in. There were houses for the 150 employees who remained with the circus through the winter months, as well as repair shops, costume rooms, and a gigantic railroad building, where the circus housed its more than 100 cars and wagons.

The mood at the winter quarters was happy and relaxed. Elephants played outside in a large, enclosed yard, their tails and ears snugly covered to protect them from the cold. Ostriches ambled freely over the property. And a constant din of excited activity filled the air. Sometimes, when the weather turned warm enough, the elephants were led a few blocks south to play in Seaside Park. To the delight of Bridgeport's citizens, Barnum himself could sometimes be seen watching his pachyderms play in the waters of Long Island Sound. Wrote one townsman, "If you come to Bridgeport in winter you will *see sights.*" Barnum agreed. "The winter quarters is where one finds the circus in its shirt sleeves," he liked to say.

BARNUM'S ELEPHANTS MARCH THROUGH BRIDGEPORT.

ONE MORNING, P. T. BARNUM received a strange letter from a man named J. A. McGonagle. "There is a rumor spreading across Iowa that you are dead," McGonagle wrote. "I am writing to find out whether this rumor is true."

Wrote Barnum in response, "My impression is that I am not dead."

But the letter, as well as his poor health, forced him to think about his legacy. What could he leave behind? How could he touch future generations? Now in old age, he decided to "do some good works," as he put it.

Bridgeport, especially, was showered with Barnum's gifts. He gave money to the city's Boys and Girls Clubs, sat on the board of the Bridgeport orphanage, contributed to the establishment of a local hospital, and even created a fund to present gold and silver medals to high school students with good public-speaking skills. Additionally, he gave thousands of books to the Bridgeport Public Library—books he picked out himself. Among the titles Barnum added to the shelves were Thomas Frost's *Circus Life and Circus Celebrities,* James Otis's *Toby Tyler, or Ten Weeks with a Circus,* and Charles Jewett's *Forty Years' Fight with the Drink Demon.* In honor of this literary contribution, the library issued him its first library card. It read simply:

P. T. BARNUM
OCCUPATION: SHOWMAN

Years earlier, Barnum had given Bridgeport a piece of land overlooking Long Island Sound that he named Seaside Park. Over time he had enlarged and improved the place, building dikes and roads and putting in statues and monuments. By the 1880s, citizens delighted in the park's beaches and gardens. They regularly flocked to the place to boat, swim, or drive their carriages along the broad boulevards, one of them named Barnum Avenue. The showman was especially proud of Seaside Park, and he expressed the hope that when people "looked across the water . . . and over the groves and walks and drives of the beautiful grounds . . . it may be a source of pride to my [family] to hear expressions of gratitude . . . expressed to the memory of their ancestor who secured to all future generations the benefits and blessings of Seaside Park." The park's 325 acres still delight visitors today.

The showman also gave the city the huge sum of $100,000 (a little over $2 million in today's money) to build a museum for the Bridgeport Scientific Society and the Fairfield County Historical Society. Called the Barnum Institute of Science and History, the museum was completed in 1893. Originally a research library and lecture hall, the museum went bankrupt during the Great Depression in the 1930s. But in 1989 it reopened as the Barnum Museum; it is devoted to telling the history of Bridgeport, the circus, and the showman himself.

As Barnum grew older, many people urged him to have a statue made of his likeness. Barnum was uncomfortable with the idea, but friends and family pressed. They commissioned noted sculptor Thomas Ball to create a monumental bronze statue of the showman. Grudgingly, Barnum agreed, but he insisted that the statue not be erected while he was still living. And he had no idea where it might be placed after his death. "Perhaps my posterity and the public will wisely conclude to bury it," he wrote. By 1888, the statue was completed and sent to a

AN ENGRAVING OF SEASIDE PARK AS IT LOOKED WHEN BARNUM FIRST ESTABLISHED IT.

A NINETEENTH-CENTURY POSTCARD SHOWS THE BARNUM INSTITUTE OF SCIENCE AND HISTORY JUST AFTER THE BUILDING WAS COMPLETED.

BARNUM'S STATUE AS IT LOOKS TODAY IN SEASIDE PARK.

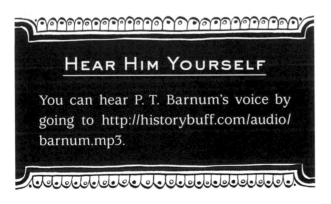

HEAR HIM YOURSELF

You can hear P. T. Barnum's voice by going to http://historybuff.com/audio/barnum.mp3.

warehouse in Hoboken, New Jersey, for storage. Barnum (along with his wife and James Bailey) journeyed there to see it for the first and only time. It was, declared the showman, "the most perfect likeness we ever before saw." Then he had it nailed back into its crate and ordered that it not be brought out until he was "moldering in the grave." The statue wasn't seen again until July 4, 1893, the day before what would have been Barnum's eighty-third birthday. It was unveiled at Seaside Park, where it remains today.

Besides his likeness, Barnum also left behind his voice.

In 1883, Barnum was invited by the inventor Thomas Edison to leave a message for posterity on a newly invented device called the phonograph that could record the human voice. Never one to miss a chance to advertise, Barnum accepted Edison's offer. He said:

I thus address the world through the medium of the latest wonderful invention, so that my voice, like my great show, will reach future generations, and be heard centuries after I have joined the great, and as I believe, happy majority.

P. T. Barnum

ONE LAST TRIP

In 1889, the Barnum & Bailey Greatest Show on Earth traveled to London. Barnum insisted on going along. At seventy-nine, he fretted that he might not make it back alive. But taking his circus to Europe was one of his most cherished dreams. "I refuse to let the aches and pains hold me back," he said.

The show opened at London's Olympia Hall on November 11 to rave reviews. European audiences had never seen anything like it. And Barnum got all the credit. "He has one idea—the show, the whole show, and nothing but the show," praised the *London Evening News and Post*. "He piles on crowds and crowds, throws in a dozen elephants here, a hundred ballet girls there with an audacity that makes him the world's greatest showman."

Barnum became the toast of the town. Banquets were held in his honor. Songs and poems were composed about him. And Madame Tussaud made a figure of him for her world-famous wax museum, which delighted him. "I am having fun," he wrote a friend.

Four months later, he returned to the United States feeling energized. The trip abroad, he told his wife, Nancy, had done him a world of good. "I eat, sleep and walk like a boy of sixteen!"

But in early November 1890, he suffered a stroke. Confined to his bed, Barnum still insisted on dressing each day and taking care of a little business. But his strength was slipping away. In March, he asked the *New York*

A PHOTOGRAPH OF BARNUM TAKEN DURING HIS LAST TRIP TO EUROPE IN 1889.

Evening Sun to do him one last favor. Could they print his obituary early so he could read it? The editors agreed. On March 24, the headline declared:

GREAT AND ONLY BARNUM
HE WANTED TO READ HIS OBITUARY;
HERE IT IS

And in the body of the text, the showman read:

> P. T. Barnum held no exalted official station, neither was he eminent in the world of politics, literature, science or art . . . He was only a showman. Yet there was [no more famous] man of his time. For fifty years he was never lost to view. Through his search for curiosities, his name became familiar . . . in far parts of the earth. No man was so well known to the youth and adults of America. His "Greatest Show on Earth" was a collection of the wonderful, the curious, and the pleasing. It grew from Barnum's brain alone. This is his eulogy, that he was a public-spirited citizen, he furnished delights to millions, he added to the sum of childhood's and of human joy.

Less than a month later, the *Sun* was forced to run the real thing. On Monday, April 7, 1891, eighty-one-year-old P. T. Barnum slipped into a coma and died.

The city of Bridgeport plunged into mourning. Businesses closed. Flags flew at half-mast. Buildings and homes were draped in black crepe. On April 10, a public funeral was conducted by Barnum's Universalist pastor. The service, however, was held at the South Congregational Church because it

This lithograph celebrated Barnum's life by depicting his many accomplishments.

THE CIRCUS MUST GO ON

You can still see Barnum's circus. Known nowadays as the Ringling Bros. and Barnum & Bailey Circus, it travels eleven months out of the year, performing for millions of families in ninety cities across the country. While the circus no longer includes a sideshow or a menagerie tent, it continues to delight audiences with fierce lions, dancing elephants, and trained dogs. Considered a national tradition, it still reflects the curiosity, amusement, and imagination of the man who helped create it well over a hundred years ago.

was the only church in Bridgeport large enough to accommodate the thousands of mourners. Among them was James Bailey, along with numerous circus employees who had traveled to Bridgeport. (Performances were canceled that day.) Afterward, the coffin was taken to Mountain Grove Cemetery, where Barnum was buried.

"The foremost showman of all time," wrote the *Boston Herald*, "is gone."

Bibliography,
Source Notes,
Picture Credits
& Index

BIBLIOGRAPHY

〰 Most of the information in this book came directly from Barnum and his seemingly endless stream of stories, pamphlets, articles, advertisements, books, and letters. While it would be overwhelming to list every source I consulted in pulling together his life story, I found the following Barnum works essential:

The Life of P. T. Barnum, Written by Himself. New York: Redfield, 1855. Sometimes this original edition of Barnum's life story reads like an adventure novel; at other times it reads like a string of jokes, anecdotes, and homilies. This autobiography provides a vivid and candid look at his childhood and early career.

Struggles and Triumphs; or Forty Years' Recollections of P. T. Barnum. Hartford, CT: J. B. Burr, 1869. This second, greatly expanded version of Barnum's autobiography added new anecdotes not published in the 1855 version. Incredibly, *Struggles and Triumphs* continued to be revised annually with appendices and supplemental chapters, updating the progress of Barnum's career and adventures until his death in 1891.

Selected Letters of P. T. Barnum, edited and with an introduction by A. H. Saxon. New York: Columbia University Press, 1983. This marvelous work brings together more than three hundred letters written by Barnum and provides a rare glimpse into the showman's private life and personal opinions.

The Wild Beasts, Birds and Reptiles of the World: The Story of Their Capture. Chicago: The Werner Company, 1896. Published five years after Barnum's death, this rollicking, adventure-filled book details the ways in which the showman gathered animals from every corner of the world.

The Humbugs of the World: An Account of Humbugs, Delusions, Impositions, Quackeries, Deceits and Deceivers Generally, in All Ages. New York: Carleton, 1865. In this book, originally published as a series of articles in the New York *Weekly Mercury,* Barnum discusses humbugs with which he was personally familiar, and in chapter two gives and defends his own definition of *humbug.*

Funny Stories Told by Phineas T. Barnum. New York and London: George Routledge and Sons, 1890. A compilation of all the humorous anecdotes that had been deleted from Barnum's autobiographies. Many of the tales found here throw new light on old subjects, such as Tom Thumb's personality. Includes Barnum's own description of his circus's visit to England in 1889–1890.

〰 In addition to Barnum's own words, three biographies were also particularly helpful. These were:

Harris, Neil. *Humbug: The Art of P. T. Barnum.* Boston: Little, Brown and Company, 1973. Harris not only explores Barnum's public career, but also provides an in-depth study of the audiences whose desires the showman anticipated and manipulated. This last was especially helpful in understanding nineteenth-century society.

Kunhardt, Philip B. *P. T. Barnum: America's Greatest Showman.* New York: Alfred A. Knopf, 1995. This entertaining and visually delightful biography sheds invaluable light on the many images related to Barnum.

Saxon, A. H. *P. T. Barnum: The Legend and the Man*. New York: Columbia University Press, 1989. Saxon is the country's foremost Barnum scholar, and his book is by far the best-researched and most up-to-date study of the showman's life. Especially useful was the author's emphasis on the private Barnum.

☙ **For a clearer understanding of the nineteenth century's acceptance of human exhibitions, I relied on three thought-provoking books:**

Brogdan, Robert. *Freak Show: Presenting Human Oddities for Amusement and Profit*. Chicago: University of Chicago Press, 1988.

Hornberger, Francine. *Carny Folk*. New York: Citadel Press, 2005.

Thumb, Mrs. Tom. *The Autobiography of Mrs. Tom Thumb (Some of My Life Experiences)*. Edited and with an introduction by A. H. Saxon. Hamden, CT: Archon Books, 1979.

☙ **Helping me grasp the role of the circus in American culture, as well as providing succinct histories, circus lingo, delightful details, and enthralling firsthand accounts, were:**

Conklin, George. *The Ways of the Circus*. New York: Harper & Brothers, 1921.

Coup, W. C. *Sawdust & Spangles: Stories & Secrets of the Circus*, 1901; reprint, Washington, D.C.: Paul A. Ruddell, 1961.

Davis, Janet M. *The Circus Age: Culture and Society Under the Big Top*. Chapel Hill, NC: University of North Carolina Press, 2002.

Durant, John and Alice. *Pictorial History of the American Circus*. New York: A. S. Barnes, 1957.

Other invaluable sources have been cited in the chapters in which they were used.

FINDING BARNUM ON THE WEB

WWW.RINGLING.COM/ACTIVITY/EMAIL/INDEX.ASPX
Allows you to "Barnumize" your e-mail, or send a "Barnumized" postcard to your friends complete with alliteration and hyperbole—just the way the showman would have written it.

WWW.LOSTMUSEUM.CUNY.EDU/HOME.HTML
A virtual re-creation of the American Museum, this fun Web site allows online visitors to look for clues to the mystery of "who burned down the museum."

WWW.LIBRARY.UIUC.EDU/BLOG/DIGITIZEDBOTW/2008/06/
THE_LIFE_OF_PT_BARNUM_1888_BY_1.HTML
At this site maintained by the University Library of the University of Illinois at Urbana-Champaign, visitors can read a later version of Barnum's autobiography.

SOURCE NOTES BY CHAPTER

"I Am a Showman." Details of the interview: Edith Tupper Sessions, "P. T. Barnum at Home," *New York Herald,* 15 March 1891. Interpretation of Barnum's life goal: Kunhardt.

That Barnum Boy. Barnum's childhood and youth: Barnum's *The Life of P. T. Barnum* and *Struggles and Triumphs;* Saxon's *P. T. Barnum;* Kunhardt.

The Apprentice Showman. Moon hoax: Saxon's *P. T. Barnum;* Kunhardt; Alex Boese, *The Museum of Hoaxes,* New York: Penguin, 2002. The world's oldest living woman: Barnum's *The Life of P. T. Barnum* and *Struggles and Triumphs;* Benjamin Reiss, *The Showman and the Slave,* Cambridge, MA: Harvard University Press, 2001. Mr. Proler: Barnum's *Life of P. T. Barnum.* Scudder's Museum: Barnum's *Life of P. T. Barnum* and *Struggles and Triumphs;* Saxon's *P. T. Barnum;* Harris; Kunhardt. History of museums: Lloyd Habley Sellers, "The American Museum from Baker to Barnum," *New York Historical Quarterly,* 45, 1959, pp. 273–287.

A Visit to the American Museum. Details and descriptions of the museum's saloons: Kunhardt; Harris; A. H. Saxon, "P. T. Barnum's American Museum," *Seaport,* 20, Winter 1986–1987, pp. 27–33; *Catalogue or Guide Book of Barnum's American Museum, New York, Containing Descriptions and Illustrations of the Various Wonders and Curiosities of This Immense Establishment,* New York: Wynkoop, Hallenbeek and Thomas, n.d.; *Sights and Wonders in New York; Including a Description of the Mysteries, Miracles, Marvels, Phenomena, Curiosities, and Nondescripts Contained in that Congress of Wonders, Barnum's Museum; also, a Memoir of Barnum Himself, with a Description and Engraving of His Oriental Villa,* New York: J. S. Redfield, 1849. Highland Mammoth Boys: Kunhardt. Josephine Clofulia: Bogdan; Hornberger. Chang and Eng: Kunhardt; Bogdan. Anna Swan: Bogdan; Hornberger. Isaac Sprague: Bogdan; Hornberger. Caught you looking: Bogdan; Hornberger. Barnum as zookeeper: Saxon's *Letters of P. T. Barnum;* Barnum's *Wild Beasts, Birds and Reptiles;* John Richard Betts, "P. T. Barnum and the Popularization of Natural History," *Journal of the History of Ideas,* 20, 1959, pp. 353–68.

Humbug! Barnum on humbugs: Barnum's *Humbugs of the World and Life of P. T. Barnum,* Harris; Saxon's *P. T. Barnum.* Individual learning: Saxon's *P. T. Barnum.* Fejee Mermaid: Barnum's *Humbugs of the World* and *Life of P. T. Barnum;* Saxon's *Letters of P. T. Barnum;* Harris. The Wooly Horse: Barnum's *Life of P. T. Barnum;* Harris. Grand Buffalo Hunt: Barnum's *Humbugs of the World* and *Life of P. T. Barnum;* Saxon's *P. T. Barnum;* Kunhardt. The cherry cat: *Struggles and Triumphs.*

A Miniature Man and a Nightingale. Tom Thumb: Barnum's *Life of P. T. Barnum* and *Struggles and Triumphs;* Alice Desmond Curtis Thumb, *Barnum Presents General Tom Thumb,* New York: Macmillan, 1954; Mertie E. Romaine, *General Tom Thumb and His Lady,* Taunton, MA: William S. Sullwold, 1976; "Death of Tom Thumb," *New York Times,* 16 July 1883. Little people in the spotlight: Alvin Goldfarb, "Gigantic and Minuscule Actors on the Nineteenth-Century American Stage, *Journal of Popular Culture,* 10, 1976, pp. 267–79. The Swedish nightingale: Barnum's *Life of P. T. Barnum* and *Struggles and Triumphs;* Saxon's *P. T. Barnum* and *Letters of P. T. Barnum;* Harris; C. G. Rosenburg, *Jenny Lind in America,* New York: Stringer and Townsend, 1851. Hans Christian Andersen: Saxon's *P. T. Barnum.* Celebrity: Harris.

The Man Behind the Curtain. His wife: Saxon's *P. T. Barnum* and *Letters of P. T. Barnum;* P. T. Barnum, "The Liquor Business: Its Effects Upon the Minds, Morals, and Pockets of Our People,"

No. 4 in *The Whole World's Temperance Tracts,* New York: Fowlers and Wells, 1854, 12 pp. His children: Saxon's *P. T. Barnum* and *Letters of P. T. Barnum;* Caroline Barnum, "Diary July 5–August 11, 1848: The Trip Across New York and Return to Bridgeport." His home: Barnum's *Life of P. T. Barnum* and *Struggles and Triumphs;* Saxon's *P. T. Barnum.* A Day in His Life: Kunhardt. "To do" list: Kunhardt. His writing: Barnum's *Life of P. T. Barnum* and *Struggles and Triumphs;* Saxon's *P. T. Barnum* and *Letters of P. T. Barnum.* City friends: Kunhardt; Charles F. Deems, "Alice and Phoebe Cary: Their Home and Friends," *Packard's Monthly,* No. 2, February 1870, pp. 49–52. Still churchgoing: P. T. Barnum, "Why I Am a Universalist," Boston: *Universalist Publishing House,* n.d., 12 pp.

ENDINGS AND BEGINNINGS. Bankrupt!: Barnum's *Struggles and Triumphs;* Saxon's *P. T. Barnum* and *Letters of P. T. Barnum;* Chauncey Jerome, *History of the American Clock Business for the Past Sixty Years, and Life of Chauncey Jerome, Written by Himself. Barnum's Connections with the Yankee Clock Business,* New Haven, CT: Dayton, 1860. The road back: Thumb; Saxon's *Letters of P. T. Barnum;* Barnum's *Struggles and Triumphs.* Old homes and new houses: Kunhardt; Saxon's *P. T. Barnum.* Welcome back: Barnum's *Struggles and Triumphs.* Politician: Barnum's *Struggles and Triumphs;* Saxon's *P. T. Barnum.* Fire!: "Burning of Barnum's Museum," *Harper's Weekly,* 29 July 1865, pp. 472–477; Barnum's *Struggles and Triumphs.* The New American Museum: Barnum's *Struggles and Triumphs;* Saxon's *P. T. Barnum;* Harris. End of political career: Kunhardt; Saxon's *Letters of P. T. Barnum.* Fire! Fire!: Barnum's *Struggles and Triumphs.* What's next?: Saxon's *Letters of P. T. Barnum.* Grandpa Barnum: Kunhardt.

CIRCUS MAN. Partnership with Coup: Barnum's *Struggles and Triumphs;* Saxon's *P. T. Barnum* and *Letters of P. T. Barnum;* Coup, "How Barnum's Circus Was Started," *New York Clipper,* 16 May 1891. Loss and love: Barnum's *Struggles and Triumphs;* Saxon's *P. T. Barnum* and *Letters of P. T. Barnum,* Alice Graham Lanigan, "Mrs. Phineas T. Barnum," *Ladies' Home Journal,* February 1891. Mayor Barnum: *Barnum's Struggles and Triumphs;* Saxon's *P. T. Barnum.* The show goes on: Harris; Saxon's *P. T. Barnum.* James Bailey: Davis; Durant; Richard E. Conovers, "James A. Bailey," Xenia, OH: by the author, 1957, 17 pp. Illness: Kunhardt. Barnum & Bailey's big show: Kunhardt; Davis. Circus history: Davis; Coup; Durant. What's in a Name?: Kunhardt; Davis.

COME TO THE CIRCUS. Description of circus: Davis; Conklin; Durant; Barnum's *Struggles and Triumphs;* Saxon's *P. T. Barnum* and *Letters of P. T. Barnum;* Kunhardt; Harris. Circus Talk: Davis; Conklin. Charles Tripp: Bogdan; Conklin. English Jack: Kunhardt. Captain Costentenus: Bogdan; Hornberger; Durant. Jo Jo: Bogden; Hornberger; Kunhardt. Lucia Zarate: Hornberger; Davis; Kunhardt. The Seven Sutherland Sisters: Kunhardt. The children's friend: Saxon's *P. T. Barnum.* Barnum vs. Bergh: Saxon's *The Letters of P. T. Barnum.* Jumbo: Barnum's *Wild Beasts, Birds and Reptiles;* Saxon's *Letters of P. T. Barnum;* Matthew Scott, *Autobiography of Matthew Scott, Jumbo's Keeper, Formerly of the Zoological Society's Gardens, London, and Receiver of Sir Edwin Landseer Medal in 1866. Also Jumbo's Biography, by the Same Author,* Bridgeport: Trows Printing and Bookbinding of New York, 1885. The circus at rest: Barnum's *Struggles and Triumphs;* Saxon's *Letters of P. T. Barnum;* "Barnum's Show in Winter-Quarters," *Harper's Weekly,* 18 February 1882, p. 101.

THE EGRESS. Good works: Barnum's *Struggles and Triumphs;* Saxon's *P. T. Barnum;* Lennie Grimaldi, *Only in Bridgeport: An Illustrated History of the Park City,* Northridge, CA: Windsor, 1986. One last trip: Wendell H. Ordway, *Olympia Gleanings: A Review of the Winter Season of 1889–90 in London, England, with P. T. Barnum's Greatest Show on Earth,* London: Walter Hill, 1890. Death: Saxon's *P. T. Barnum;* Kunhardt; Harris; Nancy Barnum, "The Last Chapter: In Memoriam, P. T. Barnum," New York: Press of J. J. Little, 1893, 19 pp.

PICTURE CREDITS

INDEX